DATE DUE

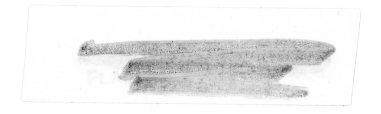

Louis Pasteur

And the Hidden World of Microbes

Owen Gingerich
General Editor

Louis Pasteur

And the Hidden World of Microbes

Louise E. Robbins

Oxford University Press
New York • Oxford

*To the memory of my grandmothers, Louise Walker Northrop
and Christine Chapman Robbins*

OXFORD
UNIVERSITY PRESS

Oxford   New York
Athens Auckland Bangkok Bogatá Buenos Aires Cape Town
Chennai Dar es Salaam Delhi Florence Hong Kong Istambul Karachi
Kolkata Kuala Lumpur Madrid Melbourne Mexico City Mumbai Nairobi
Paris São Paulo Shanghai Singapore Taipei Tokyo Toronto Warsaw
with associated companies in Berlin Ibadan

Copyright © 2001 by Louise E. Robbins
Published by Oxford University Press, Inc.
198 Madison Avenue, New York, New York 10016
www.oup.com

Oxford is a registered trademark of Oxford University Press
All rights reserved. No part of this publication
may be reproduced, stored in a retrieval system, or transmitted,
in any form or by any means, electronic, mechanical,
photocopying, recording, or otherwise, without the prior
permission of Oxford University Press.

Design: Design Oasis
Layout: Greg Wozney
Picture research: Deborah Glassman

Library of Congress Cataloging-in-Publication Data

Robbins, Louise.
Louis Pasteur : and the hidden world of microbes / Louise Robbins.
p. cm.—(Oxford portraits in science)
Includes bibliographical references and index.
ISBN 0-19-512227-5
1. Pasteur, Louis, 1822–1895—Juvenile literature. 2. Scientists—France—
Biography—Juvenile literature. 3. Microbiologists—France—Biography—Juvenile
literature. [1. Pasteur, Louis, 1822-1895. 2. Microbiologists. 3. Scientists.] 1. Title II.
Series.
Q143.P2 R56   2001
579'.092—de21   2001031405

9 8 7 6 5 4 3 2 1

Printed in the United States of America
on acid-free paper

On the cover: *Louis Pasteur in 1871.* Inset: *A painting of Pasteur in his laboratory
examining a rabbit's spinal cord, the kind used to develop the rabies vaccine in 1885.*
Frontispiece: *Louis Pasteur on the day of his induction to the Académie Française, April 27,
1882.*

Contents

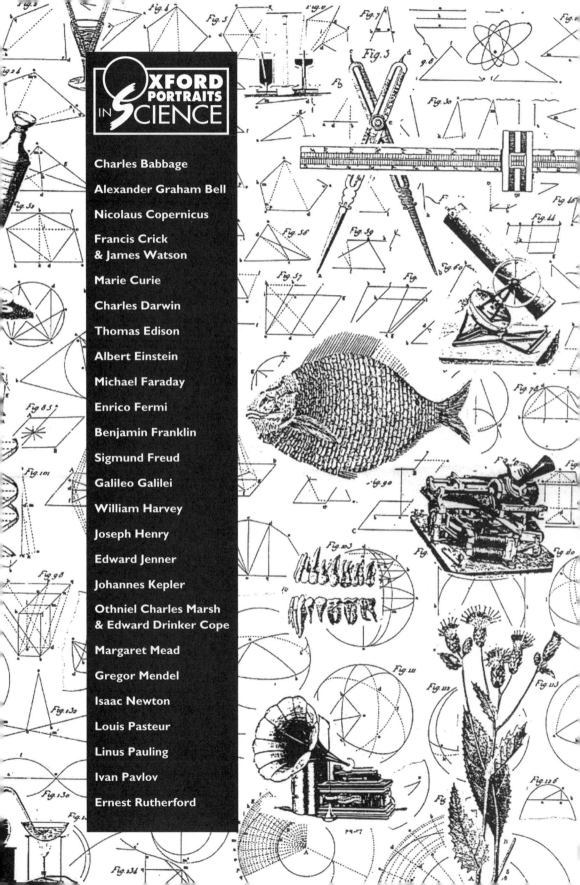

OXFORD PORTRAITS in SCIENCE

In 1886, after several American boys returned from being treated with Pasteur's rabies vaccine in Paris, they were hired as attractions at popular dime museums in New York and Philadelphia.

The Long Road to Paris

On the morning of December 2, 1885, a big, fierce dog rampaged through Newark, New Jersey, attacking everything in its path. A crowd gave chase, and someone shot it dead on the stoop of a house where it had been frantically clawing and gnawing at the door. In all, it had bitten 17 dogs and 6 children. The dog had behaved like an animal with rabies, and everyone feared that the fatal disease would spread. The city went into a panic. Bullets whizzed through the streets and hardware stores sold out of muzzles after the mayor issued an order that all unmuzzled dogs were to be shot.

If the dog had given rabies to the children it had bitten, within several weeks they would begin to develop the characteristic symptoms of the disease: fever, vomiting, convulsions, and great thirst combined with the inability to swallow (rabies was often known as "hydrophobia," or fear of water). Paralysis and death would follow inevitably. To destroy the "poison" that doctors feared had been transmitted in the dog's saliva, they performed the standard treatment, cauterization: They poured a biting solution of strong acid into the wounds (the children were spared being seared with a red-hot iron, the alternative method if no acid was handy).

Everyone knew, though, that cauterization, like other rabies remedies, often failed.

Word had recently spread, however, that the previous July, and then again in October, a French scientist named Louis Pasteur had used a new technique to save the lives of two boys who had been mauled by rabid dogs. A doctor in New York City cabled Pasteur to ask if he would treat the Newark children. Send them over as soon as possible, responded Pasteur.

A week later four of the children—William Lane (13 years old), Austin Fitzgerald (10), Patrick Reynolds (7), and Eddie Ryan (5)—boarded a steamship bound for France, along with Eddie's mother and younger brother and a New York City physician. Donations had come pouring in from working people and philanthropists alike to fund the trip. Eddie gleefully basked in the attention, but Austin, the most seriously wounded, was tormented by nightmares about mad dogs.

From news reports from Paris, Americans learned about Pasteur's laboratory and read of the boys' courage as they submitted to daily injections in the abdomen with a solution of ground-up spinal cord from rabies-infected rabbits. Americans were heartened to read in a headline in the *New York Sun* on January 15, 1886, that the children had returned the day before "plump and healthy and thankful to Prof. Pasteur." The *New York Times* described Pasteur as "a man whose lifelong studies have enabled him to deliver the innocent from certain death." A few clouds troubled the radiant praise: An editorial in the *Times* pointed out that no one knew if the children would have actually developed rabies if they had not received the inoculations, and a doctor wrote a letter to the editor stating that rabies was not a disease at all, just a name given to a collection of symptoms that resulted from many different causes.

These faint doubting voices did little to diminish Pasteur's popular acclaim. He was already renowned in France for the work he had done on the optical properties of crystals, on preventing the spoilage of wine and beer, and on the diseases of silkworms, pigs, sheep, and cattle. But with his taming of rabies, he became a worldwide hero. The dog-bitten and the wolf-bitten rushed to Paris—3 girls from Algeria, 19 men and women from Russia, and others from many different countries. Almost 2,500 had made the pilgrimage by the end of 1886, only 15 months after the first boy had been treated. In 1888 a grand research center, the Pasteur Institute, was founded in Paris as a center for rabies treatment and for research on other diseases. Pasteur became celebrated as the conqueror not just of rabies, but of disease in general.

Pasteur's life and accomplishments are easy to cast in a heroic mold. Through diligent effort, he rose to world fame from humble origins. He helped to spark a revolution in biology by proving that fermentation (the process that transforms grape juice into wine, for example) was caused by the action of tiny organisms, visible only through a microscope. Extending this discovery to medicine, he showed that these microorganisms were also responsible for many diseases in humans and animals. This concept, called the "germ theory of disease," opened up the world of bacteria and viruses that are so familiar to us today and led to the development of vaccines and antibiotics, thus saving countless lives.

But the response to Pasteur cannot be explained simply by his achievements. The reaction to his rabies treatment, for example, far outstripped its actual effects. Rabies is a rare disease that killed fewer than 100 people in France every year. Most people bitten by rabid animals do not develop the disease; most of those "saved" by Pasteur were not even doomed from the outset. The legend of Pasteur had to do with more than his considerable scientific accomplishments.

Pasteur's first biographers tended to exaggerate the heroic aspects of his life. Perhaps today's decreased optimism about the conquest of disease—in the face of AIDS (acquired immunodeficiency syndrome) and antibiotic-resistant bacteria—makes it easier to see the other side of the hero. We can admit that his success resulted from aggressive self-promotion and vigilant defense against his critics as well as from careful work in the laboratory. We can recognize that physicians who resisted his emphasis on microorganisms as the cause of disease were not ignorant, but made some reasonable arguments. And we can acknowledge that he took more risks than he admitted in his experimental work on humans. Behind the image of the savior of innocent children lies a more interesting and complicated person.

The road from tanner's son to living legend begins in a small town on the eastern edge of France. The town of Dole, where Louis Pasteur was born, lies in the province of Franche-Comté. Here, fertile valleys covered in vineyards are surrounded by wilder scenery: steep cliffs, dark forests, and the racing rivers of the Jura Mountains.

Pasteur's great-grandfather had been a serf (an unpaid laborer working for a local nobleman), but had bought his freedom in 1763 and learned the trade of "tanning," turning raw animal skins into leather. His son Jean-Henri and his grandson, Pasteur's father Jean-Joseph, had also become tanners. Jean-Joseph became acquainted with a much wider world when, at the age of 20, he was conscripted into Napoleon's army. Napoleon, a charismatic general, had taken advantage of the chaos of the French Revolution at the end of the 18th century to take power and declare himself emperor in 1804. Waging war all over Europe, he attempted to create a vast and glorious empire. Jean-Joseph fought in the brutal Spanish campaign, for which he received the honor of *chevalier* (knight) of the Legion of Honor, an award given by the French government for distinguished military or civilian service. In 1814, after Napoleon's defeat, Jean-Joseph returned to the tannery at Salins, the town where he had grown up, but he remained at heart a brave soldier. He hung his sword on the wall of the tannery between a portrait of Napoleon and another of Napoleon's son, and proudly wore his red Legion of Honor ribbon on his Sunday walks after church.

Soon after his return, Jean-Joseph courted Jeanne-Étiennette Roqui, the daughter of a gardener who lived across the river. The couple moved to nearby Dole when they married in 1816, perhaps to avoid a scandal: Jeanne-Étiennette was eight months pregnant. Their first child died after only a few months. A second child, Jeanne-Antoine (known as Virginie), was born in 1818; she and her husband would eventually take over the Pasteur tannery. Four years

The house where Pasteur was born, in Dole, backs up to the Tanners' Canal.

later, on December 27, 1822, Louis Pasteur was born. He was followed by two more sisters, Joséphine (1825) and Émilie (1826), both of whom lived only into their 20s. Pasteur liked his sisters, and he also liked lording over them. In his letters he constantly urged them to study harder and not to fight with each other. As the only son in a culture where men held the authority in public and at home, Pasteur was keenly aware of his privileged role in the family.

The Pasteurs left Dole in 1826 to live with Jeanne-Étiennette's mother in Marnoz, but a year later they moved again, to Arbois, a nearby wine-producing town, where they were to remain. They settled into a stone house on the Cuisance River, and Jean-Joseph installed pits for soaking animal skins in solutions of compounds that preserved them from rotting. Pasteur always remained nostalgic for the odors of his youth: tanning hides and fermenting grapes. Few of the townspeople would have predicted that this boy—a serious but average student, with a talent for drawing—would later set up a laboratory in Arbois where he would study the fermentation of local wines and develop a preservation process that made his name a household word: "pasteurization."

Arbois, in 1995, had not changed substantially from the time Pasteur grew up there. The town was always dear to him, and later in life he did research and spent "vacations" there—working on scientific papers and keeping up with correspondence.

At home Louis imbibed the values that would remain with him throughout his life: hard work, patriotism, and devotion to family and religion. He shared these values with many middle-class Frenchmen, but he took them so seriously that he developed into a rather humorless and pompous man, with a thick streak of sentimentality. His family, above all, aroused emotional effusions, although he often neglected them when he was involved in research projects. During a ceremony in 1883 marking his place of birth with a plaque, he paid homage to his parents:

> Oh! my father and my mother! Oh! my dear departed ones, who lived so modestly in this little house, I owe everything to you! . . . you, my dear father, whose life was as harsh as your harsh trade, you showed me what can be done with patience for sustained effort. It is to you that I owe my tenacity in daily work. Not only did you have the quality of perseverance that makes people's lives useful, but you also had admiration for great men and great things.

Louis attended the public primary school in Arbois, where he was an unremarkable student. He showed more promise during secondary school, at the Collège d'Arbois (a *collège* is roughly equivalent to an American high school), and his father began to plan an ambitious career for Louis: He would go on to earn a higher degree and then return to Arbois to be a *professeur* (schoolmaster) at the collège. Compared to his ultimate route this proposed path seems laughably ordinary. But in small provincial towns, schoolteachers were among the most respected citizens.

One of Louis's teachers, however, suggested that Louis should aim his sights higher, toward the prestigious École Normale Supérieure in Paris, the teacher-training school that admitted only France's best students. The thought appealed to Louis, who must at this time have begun to feel the pricklings of ambition that would push him so hard later on. His father agreed to send him to a private boarding school in Paris that prepared students for admission to the

École Normale. Since the director was from the same province, he charged the family reduced fees. With some trepidation, Jean-Joseph watched 15-year-old Louis, along with a school friend, board a carriage bound for Paris in October 1838. One month later, Louis was back in Arbois. He had been so homesick that he could not stand it. "If I could only catch a whiff of the tannery," he told his friend, "I would feel better."

In Arbois, Louis worked hard—drawing pastel portraits of his parents, the mayor, a nun, a barrel maker, and other local citizens. Would he have become a renowned artist if he had chosen to continue drawing instead of studying chemistry? Some critics find marks of artistic talent in the pastels; others think they display little creativity. What they certainly show, however, are qualities of observation, attention to detail, and a deft hand that served him well in the laboratory.

"Whatever situation you find yourself in," wrote Pasteur's mother to him a few months before she died, "never be unhappy; everything in life is an illusion." Pasteur drew this pastel portrait of his mother when he was 13 years old.

Pastels would not get Louis into the École Normale, the route his father and the local schoolmaster continued to urge him to take. So, in October 1839, he entered a secondary school that offered a more complete curriculum than the one in Arbois, the Collège Royal de Franche-Comté in Besançon. This time he would be closer to home. Besançon was only 25 miles from Arbois, and his father traveled there occasionally to sell hides. A few months after starting school, he wrote to his sisters (after encouraging them to work hard) "love each other as much as I love you, while waiting for the happy day when I will be admitted to the École Normale."

Eventually he achieved this goal: Five years after fleeing Paris, he was admitted to the École Normale. But it was a long and frustrating five years, during which he met continued disappointment with a remarkable stubborn persistence.

Educational reform also had something to do with Louis's success. In the previous century, workers and peasants would have had little if any schooling before beginning an apprenticeship or work in the fields. But primary education had gradually become more and more widespread. In 1820, literacy rates in Franche-Comté were about 50 percent for men and 25 percent for women; 50 years later the figures were 95 percent and 90 percent, respectively. Only a small proportion of students went on to higher levels of study, however, and at each step a ruthless public weeding process took place: Students took arduous exams and received numerical rankings indicating their performance relative to the other test-takers.

The first year at Besançon, Louis studied history, geography, philosophy, Greek, Latin, rhetoric, and sciences. He received his baccalaureate in letters in August 1840, but his examination grades were only mediocre. The next year, he concentrated on mathematics and sciences and also worked as a tutor, a job that earned him room and board and a small salary. The following summer he went into the examination for the baccalaureate in sciences with great confidence—too great, for he failed. He had to return to Besançon for one more year. He studied harder this time and received better grades in his classes but felt lonely and unhappy. He worried that mathematics was deadening his soul: "Nothing dries up the heart so much as the study of mathematics," he wrote in a letter to his parents. He hardly ever wept anymore when he read a touching story, he told them. "Well, that's life. You have to move on," he concluded pragmatically. He missed his friend Charles Chappuis, who had already gone on to Paris to study philosophy at the École Normale. Louis had met Chappuis the first year at Besançon, and they remained best friends for the rest of their lives. Louis was shy and projected reserve rather than warmth, but rays of affection shine from the letters to his few close friends and family. He wrote to Chappuis in Paris, "I have only one pleasure, that of receiving letters, either from you or from my parents. So, my dear friend, write often."

The hard year at Besançon paid off, and this time Louis passed the examinations and received the baccalaureate in sciences. But he did not do as well on the hurdle that he faced two weeks later: the entrance exams for the École Normale. A five-day ordeal, the exams included a six-hour session for working two mathematics problems. He was admitted to the school, but was ranked 15 out of 22 accepted students. Rather than begin as a second-rung student, he decided to study for one more year and then retake the exams. Paris seemed to be the best place for more advanced classes. Although his family felt anxious about sending him back to Paris—distant, dangerous, and full of temptations—they agreed.

In October 1842, now almost 20 years old, back he went to the same preparatory school that he had left so suddenly four years before. He shared a room with two other young men in a building owned by a public-bath proprietor. Louis's father liked this arrangement, urging him to bathe often, but not in overly hot water. Louis's day began at 6 A.M., when he tutored elementary students in mathematics in order to pay part of his room and board. The rest of his time was spent taking courses at the Collège Saint Louis, or attending lectures at the Sorbonne, and studying with his friend Charles. "Who do I spend time with?" he wrote to his parents, "Chappuis. Who else? Chappuis." The two friends went to a couple of plays, but otherwise they seem to have ignored the charms of Paris, much to his parents' relief. He described the city to them as "so beautiful and so ugly. . . . Here more than anywhere virtue and vice, integrity and dishonesty, fortune and misery, talent and ignorance collide and intersect. But when one has a firm character, one's heart remains simple and honest, just as in any other place."

What excited Louis most during this year was listening to lectures by the chemist Jean-Baptiste Dumas at the Sorbonne. Dumas had done important work in the foundations of organic chemistry and was also a well-known public figure: a senator and government minister. He lectured with such animation and eloquence that 600 to 700 students would crowd into the auditorium to listen.

Louis did very well in his classes, and the following summer he took the École Normale entrance examination again. This time he was ranked number four and could enter with head held high. In October 1843, he moved into the dormitory of the École Normale and started 12-hour days of lectures, study, and laboratory work.

Pasteur at age 29, when he was a professor at the University of Strasbourg.

CHAPTER 2

Crystals of Life

At the École Normale, Pasteur took courses in chemistry and physics and discovered the joy of laboratory work. The laboratory became, and remained, Pasteur's greatest love and favorite place to be. Pasteur knew that he wanted to spend his life as a research scientist, but to create such a life required a single-minded determination at a time when few people marched along that career path. Later he played a part in changing the system to make his own footsteps easier to follow.

In mid-19th-century France, the education system channeled science students into one of two major routes, both requiring education in Paris. Graduates of the École Polytechnique became government scientists who worked on applied engineering, military, or agricultural projects; graduates of the École Normale became secondary-school teachers. At best, ambitious École Normale graduates might hope to work their way up from the provinces to a teaching job at a secondary school in Paris, or to be appointed to a provincial Faculty. The Faculties, institutions for post-secondary school education, had few regular students. The professors lectured to audiences made up mostly of the general public and oversaw the baccalaureate examinations given at the secondary schools; few did research.

Like the other students at the École Normale, Pasteur prepared to take the examination for a teaching certificate. He earned spending money tutoring at Barbet's school, where he had been a student himself the year before. Sundays found him still busy: He had convinced Jean-Baptiste Dumas, the chemist whose lectures he had found so exciting, to let him work in his laboratory.

Pasteur's father continued to be proud of his son but worried about his health, constantly urging him to eat well, to dress warmly, to drink good wine, not to go out at night, and not to study too hard. He badgered him to specialize in mathematics rather than physics, because math teachers were paid better and worked fewer hours. "In my opinion, it's wrong to refuse money when you have a chance to get it, since when it is well earned, even if it can't *make* you happy, it can certainly help," he advised. To him, education was a route to a comfortable life, an escape from the labor of lifting and hauling hides, and he never quite understood his son's ambition to excel.

Pasteur's father wrote to his son at the École Normale that he had bottled some wine to drink to the school's honor. "There's more wisdom in those 100 liters then in all the philosoply books in the world. But as for Mathematical formulas, I believe there are none."

Pasteur followed his own inclinations and received his certificate in physics in September 1846, ranking third of four students who passed the exam (10 failed). He immediately received an assignment as a physics teacher at the secondary school in Tournon, a small town south of Lyon, but he did not want to go. He wanted, instead, to continue his laboratory work. He wrote to Dumas, asking if he could stay in Paris one more year. One of Pasteur's teachers, the chemist Antoine Balard, added his voice to Pasteur's plea, stating that it would be a shame to banish such a promising student. Pasteur was reprieved: He was hired as an assistant in Balard's laboratory, where he did the research that resulted in two theses, one in chemistry and one in physics, which earned him a doctoral degree in 1847. Pasteur's father remarked that he would have been content if Louis had stopped with his teacher's certificate, but he had apparently resigned himself to accept his son's choice. "So many noble young men have sacrificed their health for the love of science," he wrote. "Now I understand that you are different: your success and your work habits allow you to [pursue science] without harm." Still looking for some practical benefit, however, he passed on a friend's observation that Louis could now hope to make a brilliant marriage. He would merely have to ask and he would succeed, his friend asserted: only an idiot would refuse such a fine young man.

But marriage was not yet on Pasteur's mind. He spent his days in Balard's laboratory, where he explored an exciting new discipline, organic chemistry—the study of substances found in plants or animals. Pasteur was drawn into an area that he had found fascinating during his studies and that was also on the cutting edge of the field: crystallography. Crystals, solids that have a regular geometrical shape, are formed both by inorganic compounds like salt or water (snowflakes, for example, are water crystals) and by organic compounds such as sugar. Chemists wondered whether the structure of crystals could reveal anything about the structure of their underlying, invisible building blocks—atoms and molecules—but results so far had been inconclusive. At the suggestion of one of Balard's colleagues, Pasteur began investigating the relationship between the chemical makeup of a substance and the types of crystals it forms, focusing on tartaric acid and tartrate salts. Tartaric acid, a substance found in many fruits and vegetables, was a common byproduct of wine making; it was purified in factories from crystals that formed in vats of fermenting wine and was used in the dye industry, as well as by pharmacists, and in baking (as an ingredient in baking powder). Tartrate salts are related forms in which one of the hydrogen atoms of the acid is replaced by a mineral such as potassium or sodium.

An odd form of tartaric acid, called "paratartaric", or "racemic," acid, became the focus of Pasteur's work. Racemic acid (from *racemus*, the Latin word for a cluster of grapes) had first been isolated in 1822, and analysis had shown that it had the same chemical formula as tartaric acid. The two acids, however, displayed a striking difference in a characteristic known as "optical activity." A solution of tartaric acid was optically active, meaning that a beam of polarized light—light whose rays vibrate in a single plane—rotated when shown through it in a device called a "polarimeter." Racemic acid, however, was not optically active. Chemists expected that because the acids differed in optical activity, crystallized salts of the two acids would also differ from each other. It was a surprise when the German chemist Eilhard Mitscherlich reported to the French Academy of Sciences in Paris in 1844 that their crystalline forms were identical. Two acids with the same chemical formula and the same crystal structure: Why would they affect light differently?

Pasteur suspected that Mitscherlich was wrong and decided to look for himself at the microscopic crystals. Based on previous work by others, he guessed that racemic acid crystals would be symmetrical, that is that they would have two identical halves, like a chair, but that the tartaric acid crystals would be asymmetrical, like a chair with one missing leg. The tartaric acid crystals were indeed asymmetrical. Each one had a tiny notch in one corner, which explained why the acid was optically active. But when Pasteur peered closely at the racemic acid crystals, he saw something that no one else had noticed, and that many people had a hard time seeing even after they knew about it. The racemic acid crystals had the same general shape as tartaric acid crystals, with the same slight notch, but in some crystals the notch was on the right side, and in others it was on the left side.

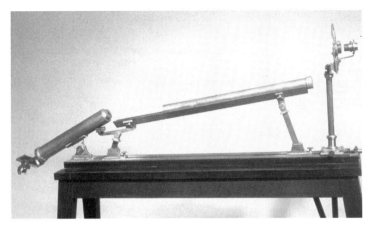

Pasteur used this polarimeter, which was invented by his mentor Jean-Baptiste Biot, to test optical activity—to see whether polarized light shone through a substance would be rotated to the left, to the right, or not at all.

After more checking and confirming, Pasteur believed that he had solved the puzzle. Racemic acid was a mixture of equal amounts of normal "right-handed" tartaric acid and a previously unknown type of "left-handed" tartaric acid that had the same chemical formula but structurally was a mirror image of normal tartaric acid. The right-handed tartaric acid was optically active, but when the right-handed and left-handed forms were mixed together to make racemic acid, their opposite effects on polarized light canceled each other out. This explained why racemic acid was optically inactive.

Pasteur, only 24 years old, had answered a question that had mystified prominent scientists for years. He became addicted to the rush of research, and from then on he could barely be pried away from the laboratory. He wrote to his friend Chappuis, "I am extremely happy and attribute my happiness to the fact that I am in the laboratory studying chemistry every day."

The work on racemic acid also brought him the attention that launched his career. Balard began to talk about his young protégé's discovery and caught the ear of the celebrated physicist Jean–Baptiste Biot, who had first discovered the optical activity of organic compounds. Biot summoned Pasteur to demonstrate his discovery. Pasteur did so right

text continued on page 29

STEREOCHEMISTRY: THE SCIENCE OF SPATIAL ARRANGEMENT

What is the three-dimensional arrangement of atoms in molecules? How is it possible to know, as they are too small to see? Despite this serious obstacle, chemists made great strides in understanding molecular structure during the 19th century, and in the 1890s the word "stereochemistry" (from the Greek word *stereo,* meaning solid) was coined to describe the study of the spatial arrangement of atoms in the structure of the molecule.

It was not at first obvious why the arrangement of atoms would be important or even if it could be studied. In the early 19th century, chemists were concerned mostly with identifying the different elements and figuring out their proportions in compound substances. It had been determined, for instance, that water was a combination of oxygen and hydrogen. Many chemists believed that theories about molecular structure lay outside the bounds of legitimate chemistry. New ideas and techniques, however, suggested ways to gain knowledge indirectly.

Crystals seemed to offer one way to peer into the hidden inner world of matter. If crystals were made of uncountably huge numbers of invisibly small particles packed together tightly, then the shape of a crystal might reveal something about the shape of the particles of which it was made. Experiments early in the 19th century using polarized light seemed to confirm this hunch. In normal light rays, the waves vibrate in all directions; in polarized light they all vibrate in the same plane—like a rope shaking straight up and down rather than all around. Pasteur's mentor Jean-Baptiste Biot discovered that when polarized light shone through quartz crystals, the plane of polarization rotated: A vertical plane of light, for instance, would emerge tilted. Sometimes the plane was rotated to the right, and sometimes to the left.

Other scientists discovered that two types of quartz crystals, both asymmetrical but mirror images of each other, had opposite effects on polarized light. These two crystal types were called "left-handed" and "right-handed," since they were like left and right hands. If you hold up a right-handed glove in front of a mirror, the reflection shows you a left-handed glove. They are identical in shape, but not interchangeable: A right-handed glove can not be worn on the left hand.

Biot then discovered that this rotating effect on light was not restricted to crystals. Some liquid solutions, but only of organic compounds such as nicotine, sugars, and tartaric acid, were also optically active, that is, polarized light rotated when shone through them. The molecular structures of these compounds could not be seen, but, making the analogy to the quartz crystals, chemists wondered if something in the arrangement of the atoms affected the light beam.

Through his studies of tartaric and racemic acids, Pasteur was the first to show the connection between optically active organic compounds and their corresponding crystals. A solution of left-handed tartaric acid crystals rotated polarized light to the left, and one of right-handed tartaric acid rotated it to the right. He suggested that their underlying molecular structures were asymmetrical mirror images of each other, although he could never prove his supposition. His further experiments on other organic acids produced much more complicated results, and the simple connection between molecular and crystalline structure did not hold. Pasteur had been extremely lucky in his choice to work on tartaric acid. What remained valid, however, was the observation that compounds in living organisms usually occur only in one form, either right-handed or left-handed.

The next milestone in stereochemistry came in 1874 when two scientists, Jacobus van't Hoff and Joseph Le Bel, working separately, both explained why organic compounds often have two mirror-image forms. It had recently been shown that carbon atoms, which are the backbone of all organic substances, can make bonds with four other atoms or groups. If all four of these are different, then they can be grouped around the carbon atom in two different arrangements that are mirror images of each other, called "stereoisomers."

After 1951, when the invention of X-ray crystallography allowed the three-dimensional structure of molecules to be determined directly, this hypothesis was confirmed. (X-ray crystallography involves passing a beam of X rays through a crystal; the pattern that results from the scattering of the beam provides information about the positions of the atoms in the crystal.)

Recent work in stereochemistry has shown how important the form of the molecule is for reactions that take place in plants and animals. Enzymes,

STEREOCHEMISTRY

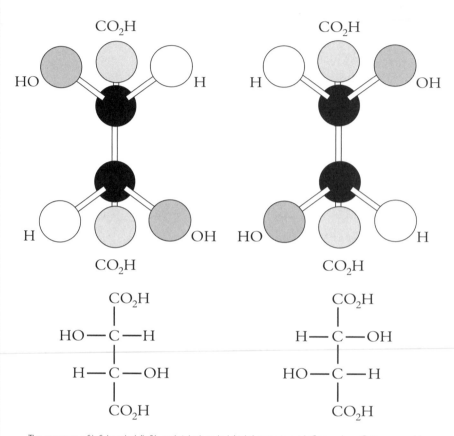

The structure of left-handed (left) and right-handed (right) tartaric acid. C = carbon, O = oxygen, H = hydrogen. Pasteur correctly hypothesized that the two forms would be mirror images of each other, but it was not until after his death that scientists were able to determine their structures.

the protein molecules that mediate chemical reactions, often recognize only one form of a compound, the right-handed or the left-handed. When pharmaceutical companies synthesize drugs, they have to make sure to manufacture the correct form to bind with the receptors in the body; the wrong form would fail to react, in the same way that a left hand does not fit a right-handed glove.

text continued from page 25

before his eyes, separating the left-handed and right-handed crystals of the racemic acid salts from each other. This demonstration had important consequences for Pasteur, for, impressed with the young man's careful experiments and logical thinking, the 74-year-old Biot took him under his wing. He helped Pasteur through the early years of his career, recommending Pasteur for jobs and giving him advice.

Acting like a wise trainer reining in an energetic young horse, Biot often advised Pasteur to tone down claims about the immense significance of his work. For example, he suggested in a letter that Pasteur change the wording in a paper he had submitted for publication from "I shall announce to the Academy a finding that deserves to command the highest degree of attention" to "which seems to me to be of considerable interest." Biot added that "one should never speak so favorably of one's own work."

On another occasion, Pasteur was desperately searching for funding so that he could travel to a factory in Saxony, a potential source of racemic acid. He asked Biot to use his influence to obtain funds from the Academy of Sciences; Pasteur was even considering asking the president of France himself, he noted in a letter to Biot. Biot replied that he would lend Pasteur the money and that Pasteur should not bother the Academy or the government, especially for a project whose results were not certain.

The year 1848 marked a turning point in Pasteur's laboratory life, and it was also a crucial year for his family and for France. Revolutions—fueled by economic hardship, workers' demands for political representation, and nationalist movements—broke out all over Europe that year. In France, a constitutional monarchy had been established in 1830 after the July revolution and the fall of

The physicist Jean-Baptiste Biot felt warm affection for Pasteur. "At my age," he wrote, "one lives only in the interest one takes in those one loves. You are one of the small number who can provide such food for my mind."

Charles X. The new king, Louis Philippe, was supposed to be king "of the French" rather than king "of France," the title of former sovereigns. His administration, however, sustained criticism for harsh laws and inattention to the miserable conditions of the people, of whom fewer than 1 percent had the right to vote. Suddenly, in February 1848, the undercurrent of revolt broke to the surface. Thousands rushed into the streets of Paris, the king fled to England, and the rebels declared a republic (the Second Republic) with voting rights for all—men, that is; women were still not allowed to vote. Pasteur reveled in the excitement, joined the National Guard, and wrote to his parents that he would happily fight for the republic. But reports of the riots, arrests, and killings frightened his family, and his father urged him to stay in his room. In May, Pasteur returned suddenly to Arbois after he heard that his mother was ill; he arrived just after she died of a stroke. He felt guilty and wondered if his mother's death had been triggered by her worrying about him.

Back in Paris, Pasteur continued his research while the political situation evolved. In December 1848, Louis Napoleon, nephew of Emperor Napoleon Bonaparte, was elected president of France, and the most radical of the Republic's reforms began to be dismantled. In 1852, following a coup d'état the previous year, Louis Napoleon became Emperor Napoleon III and the Second Empire was born. The emperor's interest in scientific and industrial progress would later greatly benefit Pasteur's research program.

While chaos still reigned in Paris, however, Pasteur's family was glad to hear that he would be leaving: He had been appointed to teach physics at a school in Dijon. He began teaching in November 1848, but soon began to complain of the long hours he had to spend preparing lessons. Only two months later, he received the happy news that he had been recommended to a higher position as a professor of chemistry at the University of Strasbourg, where he was to take the place of a professor who was on leave.

Pasteur began his sojourn in Strasbourg with a bold but practical action. On February 10, only about two weeks after he had arrived, he wrote to Charles Laurent, the head of the university, to ask for his 22-year-old daughter Marie's hand in marriage. He had probably seen Marie at a reception at the Laurent home but may not ever have spoken to her. His letter described his family background, his education, his love of science, and his ambition to be elected a member of the Academy of Sciences (he sent along a copy of a favorable report on his research from the Academy). He announced that his father would soon come to Strasbourg to make the formal marriage proposal. "P.S.," the letter concluded, "I turned 26 last December 27." The slow response to his businesslike letter must have made him wonder whether he was as eligible a bachelor as he had thought. He wrote to Marie and to her mother, acknowledging that he lacked the stan-dard charms that might attract young women. "All I ask, Mademoiselle Marie, is that you not judge me too fast: you could make a mistake. Time will show that under this cold, shy exterior that must displease you lies a heart full of affection for you." After a meeting early in April, during which Marie let Louis take her hand when they parted, he wrote to her of his fears that he would lose her and declared: "You are everything to me. I have only one thought now: you." Five days later he announced in a letter to his friend Chappuis that he was to be married. "All the qualities that I could want in a woman I find in her." Marie and Louis were married on May 29, 1849.

Pasteur could not have made a better choice. Marie looked after the family and household affairs, served as a

Marie Laurent, before her marriage to Pasteur. For 46 years, Madame Pasteur managed the household and served as her husband's secretary and confidante.

skillful secretary, and quickly discovered that even in the family the laboratory came first. She might at first have expected something different. In an early burst of enthusiasm, while he was still courting Marie, Louis told her in a letter that "my work is nothing, I who so loved crystals, I who always wished that the night would be shorter so I could begin studying earlier." But only a year and a half later we find him writing to his friend Chappuis that the nights seem too long and that Marie is scolding him for working too hard. "I console her by saying that I shall lead her to posterity," he explained.

Chappuis later told Pasteur's son-in-law a revealing story from those early years. Marie had heard that a gala parade was taking place in Strasbourg in honor of Louis Napoleon's visit, and she asked her husband to go with her to see it. "Just give me a minute to go to the laboratory, then I'll be right back," answered Pasteur. When he returned several hours later for dinner, he shrugged, "What do you want? I couldn't interrupt my experiments." Marie adapted. She learned that her activities were secondary to her husband's work: "It's simple. I never make any plans," she later told her son-in-law.

Pasteur did take time to become a father, though. The family immediately began to grow, with three children born in the first four years of their marriage (Jeanne in 1850, Jean-Baptiste in 1851, and Cécile in 1853). The children made the Pasteurs' poor financial situation even more difficult. As a replacement professor, Pasteur was paid only half of a regular professor's salary. To increase his income he agreed to teach extra courses, but he chafed at the lack of time for research. When he finally became a full professor at the end of 1852, he cut back his teaching from four to two days a week, which left him, as he remarked in a letter, five days in the laboratory. He found a few moments to play with the children in the evening, Marie reported to her father-in-law, but he did not like cleaning up "Batitim" (as he called Jean-Baptiste) when he wet his bed.

In 1852, Pasteur heard that racemic acid, which had been scarce since its first appearance in a tartaric acid factory in 1822, had appeared again. After spending a month visiting tartaric acid factories in Germany, Vienna, and Prague, he concluded that racemic acid was naturally present in certain unrefined tartars, rather than being produced by the industrial process itself.

Back in Strasbourg, he attempted to transform tartaric acid into racemic acid, a feat that seemed impossible: How can you turn right-handed gloves into pairs of gloves? But eventually he succeeded, using a process of heat and chemical treatment. He excitedly informed Biot, who reported his success to the Academy of Sciences. Pasteur, with his usual exaggeration, stated that his discovery would have "incalculable" results for industry. Despite Pasteur's prediction, racemic acid never became a product for industrial use. However, Pasteur did win a prize given for the first person to produce racemic acid artificially, and in 1853 the government made him a *chevalier* (knight) of the Legion of Honor, putting him in the same company with his father, if for a very different accomplishment.

Pasteur's early success went to his head. He wanted to achieve much more than unravel the mystery of racemic acid. He confided to Chappuis and to his father that he was on the verge of a brilliant discovery that would lift up a corner of the veil behind which God had hidden the secrets of the universe. Marie proudly wrote to her father-in-law that Louis was working on experiments that would make him another Newton or Galileo.

The secret of life? Asymmetry. Pasteur was entranced by the fact that optically active compounds—such as tartaric acid with its asymmetrical crystals—were produced only by living organisms, not in the laboratory. He theorized that asymmetrical influences such as magnetism or the earth's rotation might be at the root of the "handedness" of the compounds in living organisms. As he explained several decades later in a talk to the Chemical Society of Paris, "Life is dominated by asymmetrical actions. I can even imagine that all living species are primordially . . . functions of cosmic asymmetry." He wondered whether, if he could harness asymmetrical forces in the laboratory, he could artificially produce optically active organic compounds. If he could cross the boundary between inorganic and organic, would he in a sense have created life itself?

He tried generating crystals under the influence of magnets, and he grew plants in rooms with mirrors set up to reverse the direction of the sun's movement to see if they would produce compounds with the opposite orientation. But after months with no results, he began to despair and to suffer from headaches and stomach pains. His friends and family worried about him, and Biot wrote to him that he should not waste time and money pursuing an uncertain path, when a certain path, in which he had already succeeded and much remained to do, lay before him.

Frustrated and worn out, in early 1854 he took a leave of absence from his job and went to Paris, where he and his family stayed through the summer. He returned the following fall to Strasbourg, but not for long: He was appointed to a new position as chemistry professor and dean of the Faculty of Sciences at a new university in Lille, in northern France, to begin in December.

The position appealed to him, not only because of the salary increase and promotion, but because Lille was in the center of an industrial region, and the new university was intended to be closely allied with manufacturers and industrial chemists whose work interested Pasteur. He was thrilled when the family moved into a building whose first floor housed his laboratory, making it possible for him to go there at any hour of the day or night. It was a blissful situation for a man who had taken as his motto "Let us work, for only that provides pleasure." Following Biot's advice to give up his search for the secret of life, he began a new, less earth-shattering, but much more fruitful line of research, studying fermentation—the chemical process that converts grape juice to wine and makes milk become sour.

A year after Pasteur moved to Lille a seat became available in the Academy of Sciences, and Biot suggested that he put in his name as a candidate. The Academy, an honorary organization that held meetings in an imposing building in central Paris, comprised 66 elected members, the cream of science in France. Members enjoyed the esteem that went along with official recognition. Pasteur announced his candidacy, compiled a list of his papers and honors, and spent several weeks in Paris paying visits to Academy members and mobilizing friends to speak in his favor. Despite extensive lobbying, Pasteur lost. His reaction reveals two character traits that ultimately helped make him a success: He met disappointment with renewed energy, and he belittled anyone who opposed him. He explained to his family and friends that he had not really cared if he were elected or not, that the attempt had made his work better known, and that all the really good scientists had voted for him. Those who had voted against him, he wrote to his wife, were idiots, do-nothings who had gained entry to the Academy through luck or wealth. "I will fight with anger in my heart," he vowed to Marie.

The Pursuit of Infinitesimally Small Beings

Milk sours, bread dough rises, leaves decay, and meat rots. Unlike inorganic materials such as iron, rocks, and water, which can persist almost unchanged for centuries, organic materials, those derived from plants and animals, are constantly transforming. When Pasteur turned to the study of one of these organic processes, fermentation, he found fascinating problems to work on and the acclaim he desired; he also ruffled feathers with his new ideas and supremely confident attitude.

Pasteur's first paper on fermentation, presented in 1857 in Lille and then at the Academy of Sciences in Paris, described the process that makes sweet milk become sour: the conversion of milk sugar, or lactose, into lactic acid. The paper caused a stir because it claimed that lactic fermentation was not a chemical decay process, as most people believed, but was brought about by the action of tiny organisms so small they could barely be seen under the microscope. Three years later, Pasteur had a lengthy article

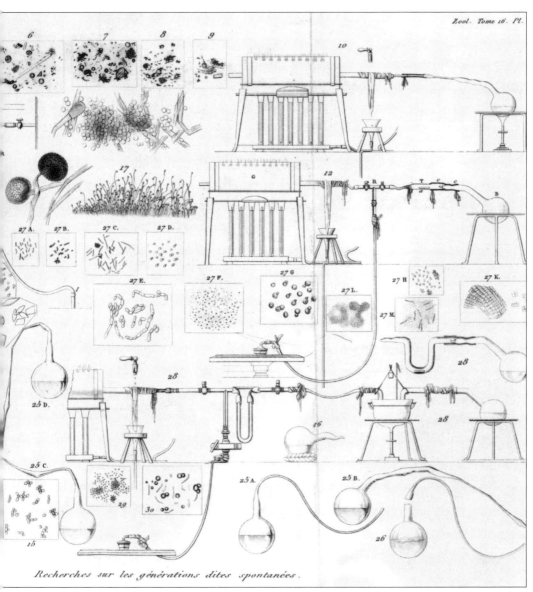

Recherches sur les générations dites spontanées.

Pasteur's studies on spontaneous generation, summarized in this diagram from an article he published in the Annals of Natural Sciences, helped to cement the idea that decay and fermentation are primarily caused by the actions of microscopic organisms.

published that extended this conclusion to alcoholic fermentation (the process that produces wine and beer). "The chemical act of fermentation," he wrote, "is essentially a phenomenon correlative with a vital act. . . . I do not think there is ever alcoholic fermentation unless there is simultaneously organization, development, and multiplication of globules [microorganisms]."

Although it sounds innocent enough today, in 1860 this was a bold statement for a young scientist to make. With it, Pasteur threw himself into a subject that had attracted prominent chemists and physiologists and positioned himself on the unpopular side of a controversy about the cause of "fermentation." Nineteenth-century scientists used the term fermentation to refer to the breaking down of sugar and other organic matter into alcohol or acid, and carbon dioxide gas. In wine making, for example, the sugar from grapes is converted to alcohol and to carbon dioxide that escapes as frothy bubbles. Bakers and brewers added yeast to initiate bread and beer production, but wine and cheese makers usually added nothing; the fermentations happened on their own.

By the time Pasteur started working on the problem, there were two theories, one chemical and one biological, about what causes these transformations. The biological theory held that fermentation was caused by microorganisms— microscopic plants or animals. In the 1830s, one French and two German scientists had independently reported that yeast was a living plant, consisting of little globules that reproduced by forming buds that broke away from the parent cell. Because yeast played a role in only some types of fermentations, however, this observation did not seem to imply any general rule about the connection between microorganisms and fermentation.

Most scientists preferred the alternative, chemical, explanation championed by the prominent German scientist Justus von Liebig, who had done fundamental work in plant and animal nutrition. Liebig stated that fermentation was a chemical process stimulated by decaying organic material. Yeast cells, like any other "ferments," could transfer their instability to other materials with which they came into contact and thus stimulate fermentation, but they did not cause it. This theory had the added benefit of fitting in with the scientific fashion of the day, which was to explain biological processes in terms of chemical reactions. It seemed unnecessary and even silly to claim that tiny organisms were masterminding these large-scale organic transformations.

Pasteur took a sidestep away from his crystal studies when he began work on fermentation, but it was a connection between the two areas, as well as exposure in Lille to large-scale fermentation of beetroot sugar into alcohol, that pushed him to make that step. In his studies on crystallization, Pasteur had proposed that only living beings produce asymmetrical molecules, that is, molecules that are optically active, bending polarized light either to the right or to the left. His former teacher and mentor, Biot, had discovered that one form of amyl alcohol, a common product of alcoholic fermentation, was optically active. If amyl alcohol is optically active, thought Pasteur, then it must be a product of a life process, not simply a chemical one.

Beginning with this hunch, he then conducted a series of experiments on lactic fermentation that culminated in his 1857 report, presented to the Academy of Sciences only eight months after it had rejected his bid to become a member. The report gave a big boost to the biological theory of fermentation, because Pasteur identified a previously unobserved microorganism, which he called "lactic yeast." This organism was much smaller than the yeast involved in alcoholic fermentation, and Pasteur probably would not have noticed it if he had not been looking for it. (The "lactic yeast" was later identified as a bacterium, a kind of one-celled organism with a simpler structure than yeast.) He presented strong evidence that this microorganism was not just associated with the fermentation but actually caused it: When he purified the lactic yeast and added it to a sugar solution, lactic fermentation began. Directly criticizing Liebig's theory, Pasteur concluded that "fermentation is connected with life and the organization of cells, not with the death or putrefaction of these cells."

Pasteur continued to work on fermentation for 20 years and to extend and solidify the generalizations he had proposed in his first studies on lactic and alcoholic fermentation. He studied many different kinds of fermentations, including alcoholic (resulting in wine and beer), acetic (resulting in vinegar), and butyric (responsible for the rancid flavor of spoiled butter). He concluded that each was produced by a different microorganism with different nutritional requirements. His demonstration that fermentation could occur in the absence of decaying organic material constituted the strongest argument against Liebig's chemical theory. Pasteur never stopped repeating his doctrine: Fermentation is caused by the vital processes of living organisms; and, like a dog guarding a bone, he attacked anyone who questioned this view, a view, in fact, that subsequent research has not completely sustained.

A number of critics raised objections and announced conflicting experimental results; the experiments and their interpretations were not as clear-cut as Pasteur liked to claim. One problem was caused by technical difficulties. Microorganisms could be hard to distinguish from nonliving

In this illustration of a drop of wine, magnified 400 times, Pasteur identified the oval-shaped organisms as the beneficial yeast responsible for alcoholic fermentation; the long, thin organisms as contaminants that made wine spoil; the long, thin crystals as a type of potassium tartrate; and the larger crystals as a type of sodium tartrate.

MALADIE DES VINS TOURNÉS.

Fig. 8.

P. Lackerbauer, ad nat, del.   Imprimerie Impériale.

400/1

a, a, Ferment ordinaire alcoolique du vin.
b, b, Cristaux aiguillés de bitartrate de potasse.
c, c, Cristaux de tartrate neutre de chaux.
d, d, Filaments du parasite qui détermine la maladie des vins tournés.

P. 59-53.

particles. They behaved differently in different circumstances and even changed shape. They snuck into flasks and beakers, where even a single cell of a wrong type could ruin an entire experiment. Aside from these issues, considerable evidence suggested that fermentation sometimes proceeded without the action of microorganisms.

Pasteur's work was generally well accepted within official scientific circles, though, and the Academy of Sciences awarded him two prizes for his work on fermentation, one in 1859 and one in 1861. He earned recognition in wider government and social circles, too, by drawing out the broader implications of his work in letters and public lectures. His goal, he wrote in 1862 in a letter to the minister of public instruction, was "the pursuit, by means of rigorous experimentation, of the physiological role, immense, in my opinion, of infinitesimally small beings in the economy of nature." At an evening lecture at the Sorbonne in Paris to the upper crust of Parisian society, he painted an intriguing picture of an alien world. Invisible microorganisms are all around us, he explained, carrying on the crucial job of converting dead matter into simple minerals and gases that can be taken up and used again by living plants and animals. If not for them, the world would fill up with dead organic matter and life would be impossible. In a letter to his father, he declared that his lectures to a distinguished audience at the Chemical Society in Paris had received an enthusiastic reception: "Everyone was struck by their importance," he wrote. Although he denied any personal vanity, claiming to care only about the advancement of science, he clearly enjoyed the attention.

Pasteur had started his fermentation studies in Lille, where he had observed the process not only in his lab, but also on an industrial scale, in the local factories that produced alcohol from sugar beets. "Louis is submerged up to the neck in beet root juice," wrote Madame Pasteur to her father-in-law. "He spends his days in an alcohol factory....

He teaches only one class per week, giving him lots of time, which he uses and abuses, I assure you." Although Pasteur liked his position in Lille, he knew that the only place from which he could advance professionally was Paris. When he found out about a job opening at the school that he himself had attended, the École Normale Supérieure, he immediately applied for it. He was accepted, and the Pasteur family moved into apartments in the school in 1857. The position as school administrator and director of scientific studies required him to oversee science instruction as well as living conditions and discipline for both science and literature students. He was not supplied with a laboratory; any research was to be done on his own time. At first he set up a lab in two small attic rooms, but after a year he convinced the director to let him use a small, detached building. He was not given a budget, but had to ask for money every year.

Pasteur used his "leisure" time very effectively to continue his experimental work. He recruited and encouraged promising students, several of whom carried on his research program, and he changed the system at the École Normale so that more students could stay on as researchers. He also founded and edited a scientific journal that published articles written by students and graduates of the École Normale, the *Annales scientifiques de l'École normale*. Pasteur's innovations were part of a wider trend in the system of higher education, which was shifting from an emphasis on training teachers to one on training researchers.

If Pasteur excelled at his unofficial job, however, he fumbled badly in his official position as school disciplinarian. Rigid and authoritarian, he harshly enforced the school's strict rules and alienated the students, especially the politically liberal literature students. Students complained when Pasteur expelled two of them for smoking and when he declared that a vile mutton stew they refused to eat would continue to be served for dinner once a week—except to those who had behaved themselves.

These incidents culminated in an outright rebellion that resulted in the replacement of the top three administrators of the school, including Pasteur, in 1867. The rebellion was set in motion when a student wrote a letter of support to a liberal senator who had publicly defended freedom of thought. A Paris newspaper got hold of the letter, which 80 students had signed (21 had refused), and published it. Because school regulations forbade any political activity, the letter-writer was suspended. Not content to leave the matter there, Pasteur demanded to know the names of the students who had leaked the letter to the press so that they could be expelled. The students refused to bend to his iron law: They walked out, and the school was forced to close. Only delicate negotiations and a change in the administration convinced them to return the following fall. After losing his job, Pasteur was given a position as chemistry professor at the Sorbonne, one of the most prestigious Parisian colleges, where he would no longer have to discipline unruly students.

The École Normale Supérieure (right) in Paris, where Pasteur spent several years as a student and 10 years as an administrator.

Pasteur's family experienced major changes during the period when he was administrator of the École Normale. In 1858, one year after he took the position, Marie bore their fourth child, Marie-Louise. The youngest ones stayed at home in the Paris apartment, while Jeanne and her brother, Jean-Baptiste, attended boarding schools in Arbois, where Pasteur had grown up and where his father and sister's family still lived. When he had time, Pasteur wrote to them. He scolded Jean-Baptiste for receiving grades of "pretty good," remarking that he should be trying for "good" or "very good." He reminded Jeanne to be obedient and polite, to be careful with her spelling and grammar, to love and fear God, and to remember to wear the apparatus that was supposed to straighten her teeth. In the summer of 1859, bad news reached Paris: Nine-year-old Jeanne had come down with a severe fever and was bedridden and unable to talk. Madame Pasteur hurried to Arbois to be with her and wrote daily letters informing her husband of Jeanne's condition. Pasteur, busy supervising exams, hoped Marie and Jeanne would soon be able to return to Paris. He was sure that after they came home he would regain his energy and once again be able to utter his habitual refrain: "One must work. We will work." At the end of August, Jeanne's fever diminished and she seemed to be out of danger. Three weeks later, however, she was dead.

The family never forgot their sorrow for Jeanne, but they were cheered by the birth of a new baby, Camille, in 1863. Their joy did not last very long. When she was two, they discovered that she had a liver tumor. Pasteur was "stunned with sadness" at this affliction against which "science is completely powerless." Just before she died, after a two-month illness, she kept asking her father to hold her cold hands in his, to warm them. Pasteur's own beloved father had died earlier that summer. In a long letter to Marie, Louis remarked that his father had not had high ambitions for him, but then, seeming to contradict himself, claimed that his father had been very proud of his accomplishments. "Ah, my poor father! I am indeed happy to have been able to give you some satisfaction," he concluded. One of Pasteur's biographers, Patrice Debré, has suggested that Louis might have been trying to justify himself for being more devoted to science than to his family.

Family tragedies did seem to spur Pasteur on. He longed to plumb the mysteries of life, death, and disease, and he became even more keenly aware of the limited time he had. He was so driven that 24-hour days were not long enough. In a letter to Colonel Favé, aide-de-camp of Napoleon III, thanking Favé for providing money for his research on wine, he complained about having to waste time on administrative tasks. He explained that a scientist has only 20 to 25 productive work years, and so he had "not a minute to spare."

Marie Pasteur holds Camille, the Pasteurs' fifth child. Although a robust-looking baby, Camille, soon developed a fatal liver tumor.

He exclaimed in a letter to an editor explaining why he must decline his request to write an article, "The life of a scientist is so short! So numerous are the mysteries of nature, especially of living nature!"

Pasteur's zeal paid off as he continued to make intriguing discoveries and earned growing acclaim from both the scientific community and the larger public. After one more unsuccessful try in 1861, he was elected to the Academy of Sciences (with 36 votes out of 60) in December 1862. After his election, Pasteur continued to explore the fermentation of wine and vinegar. Through his work and that of several other scientists, a new vision of nature emerged, one that is so taken for granted in the Western world today that it is hard to imagine any alternative view. Pasteur's strong advocacy of the biological theory of fermentation, even though incorrect in some respects, played a central part in showing the importance and ubiquity of bacteria, fungi, and other microorganisms not only as agents of fermentation but as agents of disease. Pasteur would later venture into the realm of disease, but first he turned to the subject of the origins of these microorganisms.

The topic of spontaneous generation—whether living organisms can emerge from nonliving matter—arose naturally from his theories about fermentation. Some scientists believed that yeasts and other microorganisms were generated directly from fermenting matter. Pasteur disagreed, claiming that yeasts were produced from other yeasts—that microorganisms had "parents" just like all other plants and animals. Provoked by the naturalist Félix Pouchet's arguments in favor of spontaneous generation, Pasteur set out to prove that life could not arise from dead matter. Despite what he claimed to be unassailable results, the debate carried on fiercely for decades. Pasteur's mentors believed that he spent too much time involved in this controversy, but he found it impossible to ignore challenges to his views.

text continued on page 50

Although pests like mice, cockroaches, and mosquitoes sometimes seem to materialize out of thin air, by the 18th century just about everyone agreed that they were born from parents of the same species, not from muck or swamp water. The origin of intestinal parasites and of microorganisms like yeasts, however, was not so clear. Experiments concerning microorganisms in the late 18th and early 19th centuries had been inconclusive. A common type of experiment was to take meat broth or some other material that spoiled easily, boil it until any living organism that might have been in it had died, and then see if microorganisms appeared. Sometimes they did, sometimes they did not.

When Pasteur began to study microorganisms and their relation to fermentation, he came face-to-face with the question of "spontaneous generation." Where did the microorganisms come from? Were they generated as a result of fermentation or putrefaction (decay), as many chemists claimed, or did they originate from the external environment, like seeds planted in a field? Proponents of spontaneous generation contended that living organisms could arise from nonliving material. The most common form of this viewpoint, called "heterogenesis," held that only organic matter (decayed tissue from plants or animals) could undergo this transformation.

The impetus for Pasteur's study came in 1858–59, when Félix Pouchet, director of the natural history museum in Rouen, presented a paper to the Academy of Sciences and then published a book, *Heterogenesis,* in which he argued that "proto-organisms" could be spontaneously generated. The following year, the Academy announced an award for experiments that shed light on the problem. Pasteur took up the challenge and presented a report, entitled "Memoir on Organized Corpuscles that Exist in Suspension in the Atmosphere: An Examination of the Doctrine of Spontaneous Generation." The report, which earned him the Academy's prize, shot down all of Pouchet's arguments and was intended to be a deathblow to the doctrine. Instead, Pouchet and two colleagues, along with several other scientists, countered Pasteur's arguments. Pasteur answered right back. The controversy continued through the 1870s and 1880s, when French scientists and later an English physician challenged both Pasteur's fermentation theory and his critique of spontaneous generation.

This criticism might seem puzzling, since, at first, Pasteur's experiments look unassailable. He boiled nutrient broths, sealed them in flasks with sterilized air, and no life appeared. When he then dropped in a bit of cotton that air had filtered through, microorganisms grew; Pasteur concluded that they floated along with dust in the air and had been trapped in the cotton. To counter the argument that the sterilized air in the flasks kept life from organizing itself in the nutrient broth, Pasteur placed the broth in flasks whose necks he extended into long s-shaped swan necks. The necks trapped dust and microorganisms but allowed air to flow in and out. When the flask was tilted so that this dust could enter, the broth soon swarmed with life. In response to critics who complained that boiling the broths destroyed their life-producing properties, Pasteur filled flasks with blood or urine extracted directly from dogs' veins and bladders, respectively; neither showed any alteration for months when kept in sealed flasks.

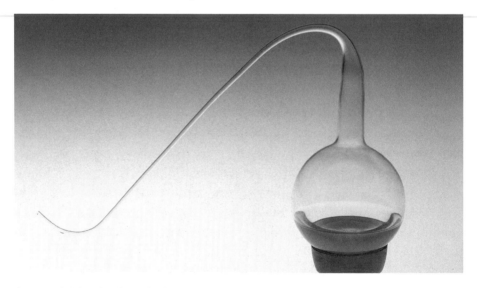

A swan-necked flask from Pasteur's laboratory, now held at the Pasteur Institute in Paris.

Venturing out from the laboratory to the mountains, Pasteur performed a dramatic experiment intended to respond to critics who ridiculed the idea that air was full of microorganisms floating around ready to fall into any open flask. Actually, some air is free of these living things, he claimed. He took sealed flasks to a glacier in the Alps, exposed them to the air, closed them up again, and brought them back to the laboratory. Only 1 out of 20 had become contaminated, in contrast to 8 out of 20 exposed at lower elevations and all 11 of those exposed in the courtyard near his laboratory.

His critics had answers for everything. They contended that he had created conditions that made heterogenesis impossible. They performed their own experiments that produced different results. Pouchet even traveled to the Pyrenees Mountains, where he exposed sterilized flasks to the pure mountain air and found that every one of them developed microorganisms. The English physician Charlton Bastian found living things growing in boiled urine. Everywhere he turned, Pasteur had new results to fight against.

Why did spontaneous generation evoke such prolonged and fierce debates? There are several reasons. First, religious beliefs about the creation of life swayed people's opinions. Second, it is difficult to prove that something can *not* happen. Defenders of spontaneous generation had only to present one positive case to support their view. Third, the experiments required great technical skill; the slightest carelessness could introduce an invisible organism into sterile broth. Finally, many aspects of microorganisms were not well understood. Pouchet's experiment in the mountains had indeed been well carried out, but for broth he used boiled hay. It was discovered later that the bacteria that infest hay can survive even when boiled for hours. Bacteria could even be carried into flasks with the water used to wash them and, in a dried state, resist boiling. Modern techniques of sterilization, in fact, derive from these discoveries. The theory of spontaneous generation eventually disappeared as a result of Pasteur's work along with improved microscopes, better understanding of cell structure and division, and research on the life cycles of intestinal worms.

text continued from page 46

Pasteur's ideas about the role of microorganisms had practical consequences in the manufacturing of vinegar, beer, and wine. In studying vinegar, he confirmed a German researcher's identification of a microorganism that transformed the alcohol of wine into the acetic acid of vinegar, and he proposed techniques for encouraging this microorganism while discouraging others that caused vinegar to spoil. Wine was also subject to spoilage. Today, waiters pour a sip of wine for their customers to taste to be sure the wine is good, and it almost always is. In the mid-19th century, though, people often encountered bitter, cloudy, or slimy wine. The control of spoilage was especially urgent after 1860, when France signed a free-trade act with England, and farmers and merchants anticipated increased foreign sales. Pasteur began a study of wine diseases in 1863. He and several of his students spent a month each fall for three years in Pasteur's home town, Arbois, the center of the Jura wine-producing region. There, and later back in Paris, they examined spoiled wine, stored bottles under different conditions, and tested preservation techniques.

Studies on Wine summarized Pasteur's research on the microorganisms that cause wine to go bad and on the use of heat to preserve it.

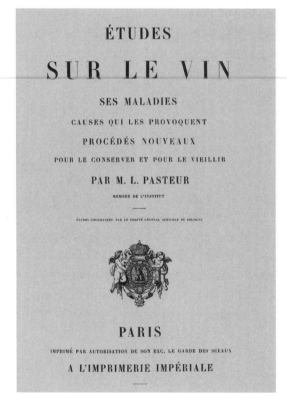

In his *Studies on Wine,* published in 1866, Pasteur explained that diseased wine was infected with unwanted microorganisms. To keep wine from spoiling, the yeast that produced the initial transformation of grape juice to wine had to be encouraged, while other microorganisms that created bad-tasting products had to be killed or discouraged. Pasteur tried adding chemicals to the wine but was concerned that they affected the taste. He then found that if the finished wine were heated to 50–60 degrees centigrade for an hour, the development of the harmful microorganisms could be significantly reduced. To counter arguments that this process gave the wine a "cooked" taste, he convened panels of specialists to compare untreated with heat-treated wines; in almost all cases, they preferred the heated wine. This process became known as "pasteurization," thus turning Pasteur's name into a household word. Later it was applied to milk, cheese, beer, and other products that are vulnerable to spoilage. Wine specialists today no longer favor pasteurization, and most wine is preserved with chemicals (sulfites). Much French cheese also remains unpasteurized and so cannot be imported into the United States. Cheese-makers and certain gourmets claim that pasteurization destroys the delicate and complex flavors of the best cheeses.

Louis and Marie Pasteur in the courtyard of the house near Alès, where Pasteur conducted research on silkworm diseases. Pasteur is dictating to Marie.

Master of the Corpuscle Disease

"Consider, I pray you, that I have never even touched a silk-worm," replied Pasteur, in 1865, when his patron and former teacher Jean-Baptiste Dumas asked him to head a commission to investigate an epidemic that was devastating the silk industry in southern France. A month later he had not only touched many worms but had begun a full-scale investigation.

Embarking on a project of interest to the French government satisfied Pasteur's patriotic feelings, and it also strengthened ties that would be crucial for his future work. Like all scientists, Pasteur needed money to support his research. The source of those funds from 1851 through 1870 was the Emperor Napoleon III, who had a strong interest in improving French industry and agriculture. Pasteur frequently asked the emperor or his aides for financial support, always emphasizing the practical importance of his studies. By the time the empire fell in 1870, Pasteur had firmly established himself as an eminent national figure.

Pasteur's introduction to the imperial inner circle came in 1865 during a weeklong house party at one of the emperor's country estates, to which he had been invited as a promising young scientist. He wrote excitedly to his wife about dining in style with dignitaries, accompanying hunting parties, and speaking to the imperial couple—whom he found utterly charming—about invisible organisms. The highlight of the visit came when he set up his microscope and showed the emperor and empress examples of disease organisms swarming in spoiled wine, including some bottles from their own fine wine cellar.

The emperor was pleased with Pasteur not only for his studies of wine, which Pasteur dedicated to him, but because he had recently agreed to take on the silkworm problem. Shortly after Dumas asked Pasteur to investigate the epidemic, in May 1865, he agreed, on the conditions that he be allowed to take several students along and that Dumas keep the mission secret—in case it failed. The project continued for the next five years and presented him with unexpected difficulties in understanding what ailed the worms and also in dealing with sometimes hostile breeders of silkworms.

The silk industry had become established in the Mediterranean region during the Middle Ages, when silkworms and their only food, mulberry trees, were brought to Europe from their native home in China. Silk producers raised the "worms" (actually caterpillars) in special breeding chambers. After the last of several molts (the process of shedding the outer covering and developing a new, larger one), the worms voraciously ate mulberry leaves in a stage called the "big gorge." Then they spun delicate cocoons of soft silk; inside they were transformed into chrysalises, the intermediate stage between caterpillar and adult. Those kept for breeding emerged as adult moths, mated, and laid eggs. The rest were killed, and their cocoons were sold for processing as silk fiber.

By the mid-19th century, France supplied one-tenth of the world's silk, producing 26,000 tons of cocoons per year. Production plummeted to less than one-sixth of this amount by 1865, however, as a result of an epidemic that spread throughout Europe and the Middle East. Silk producers had to buy eggs from Japan, the only place where healthy worms still existed, and even they did not remain healthy long. Because the sick worms were covered with black spots, the disease was called *pébrine,* from a local term for pepper. Italian researchers had discovered that the diseased worms contained microscopic particles, or corpuscles, and contended that they caused the disease, but no one had been able to consistently breed disease-free worms.

During the 1865 season, Pasteur established headquarters outside Alès, Dumas's hometown, where he and his helpers rented a house and began breeding silkworms. He stayed for only a month, interrupted by his father's funeral, then returned in the summer to Paris to the illness and death of his daughter Camille. The following winter, and each year through 1869, he returned to Alès for several months. The researchers reared worms and tried to keep the mice from eating them, picked masses of mulberry leaves for the big gorge, performed experiments and meticulously recorded the results, and peered through the microscope for hours at a time. Pasteur ran the silkworm project the same way he ran his laboratory. He worked in silence, telling his assistants what experiments to do and what data to collect, but never explaining the larger goals of the study or what hypotheses he was testing (they made a game of trying to guess). He preferred to work everything out in his own head and to announce the results in public only after the mists of uncertainty had cleared.

During the spring of the second year at Alès, two new assistants arrived to help with the study: Madame Pasteur and their seven-year-old daughter, Marie-Louise. Their arrival followed the latest in the series of family tragedies. In April 1866, Marie had taken her two daughters to eastern France to visit her brother-in-law. There, 12-year-old Cécile had come down with a fever. When the illness became grave, Pasteur took two weeks from his silkworm studies to be with her. Although she seemed to be

Pasteur's daughter Cécile (center) died of typhoid at age 12. Only two of the Pasteurs' five children, Marie-Louise (left) and Jean-Baptiste (right), survived to adulthood.

improving, Pasteur feared the worst and groaned in a letter to his wife after he had returned to Alès, "Our dear children will thus die one after another." She did die, at the end of May, and the grieving Marie brought Marie-Louise, the last of their four daughters, to join Pasteur while their son Jean-Baptiste remained in school in Paris. Both Mother and daughter thought the worms disgusting, but "Zizi" (Marie-Louise) liked going into the hills to harvest mulberry leaves. Marie spent her days plucking and sorting cocoons. In the evenings she wrote reports and letters that Louis dictated to her.

By the end of the 1866 season, Pasteur believed he was close to solving the silkworm problem. He and his team had found that moths with *pébrine* transmitted the disease to their eggs, but that the corpuscles were often visible only in the adult moths. That is, seemingly healthy worms could produce diseased eggs. The only reliable way to tell which worms had the disease was to wait until they developed into adult moths and then microscopically examine their tissues. Pasteur proposed a sorting scheme for producing healthy eggs, which he announced to silk breeders. When breeding moths emerge from their cocoons, have each one lay her eggs on a separate piece of cloth. Keep the moth and examine her tissues: If there are corpuscles, destroy all the eggs; if there are none, then the eggs will produce healthy worms. Many breeders tried this technique, as did Pasteur. "I have mastered the corpuscle disease," he boasted. "I can give it or prevent it at will."

His confidence was premature, however. Sometimes the supposedly healthy offspring died before producing cocoons, despite being free of corpuscles. This observation was very troublesome: If the disease did not always produce corpuscles, how could it be detected? Just when Pasteur thought he had solved the problem, he had to return to the drawing board. "This is not pleasant," he wrote in a letter to the minister of public instruction, Victor Duruy, requesting funds to return to Alès for another year, "but what is pleasure when one has already experienced such great sorrows by the age of 44? Happiness now exists only in searching for truth in one of its many forms."

In 1867, Pasteur finally realized what was going on. There were two different diseases: The sick worms with no corpuscles were suffering from a disease called *morts-flats* (flabby death), or *flacherie.* Once he and his assistants could distinguish between *pébrine* and *flacherie,* the team made progress in understanding both diseases. The corpuscles, Pasteur concluded, were not the symptom, as he had thought, but indeed the cause of *pébrine.* They were parasitic microorganisms that invaded the worms but became visible only when widespread throughout the tissues. Another researcher, Antonie Béchamp, had already discovered the nature of the disease, but few today remember his name.

When he began to study *flacherie,* the second disease, Pasteur found himself on more familiar, though more complex, ground. The stomach of a worm suffering from

Pasteur inspecting silk-worm cocoons with a magnifying glass. Although this drawing emphasizes the importance of the scientist, the women and men who cultivated silkworms had much practical knowledge.

flacherie was full of gas and swarming with bacteria: It looked like nothing so much as a mini–fermentation chamber. Pasteur concluded that this highly contagious disease was often transmitted when the worms ate mulberry leaves that had begun to ferment. If silk breeders looked through the microscope at the stomachs of the chrysalises and discarded those full of bacteria, they could limit the spread of the disease. This method was not as reliable as that for *pébrine*. *Pébrine* existed only in the insects, so that if sick worms were eliminated the disease disappeared. The microorganisms responsible for *flacherie,* on the other hand, always seemed to be lurking in the environment, ready to infect any breeding chamber that was too humid, too crowded, or supplied with moist mulberry leaves. Ridding silkworms of both diseases, then, required examining chrysalises and mature moths with a microscope as well as keeping the breeding chambers clean and well aerated. Even though Pasteur's team had not found a way to cure the diseases, they did believe they had discovered surefire techniques to prevent them.

Pasteur was forced to slow the frenetic pace of his work on silkworms and fermentation at the end of 1868, when, at only 45, he suffered a stroke. He had just returned from a session at the Academy of Sciences in Paris when his left side became stiff and he could not move it. Doctors bled him with leeches applied behind his ears, and the paralysis diminished somewhat, but many, including Pasteur himself, thought death had come. However, it had not, and he recovered, slowly, although his left hand remained partially paralyzed, and other symptoms continued to plague him. Only three months later he returned to Alès with his wife and daughter. Unwilling to turn the silkworm studies over to his students, he continued to direct experiments, although he remained weak and tired. He was both exasperated and touched that Zizi tried to keep him from overwork by taking away his books, papers, and pens.

In the fall of 1869, thanks to the emperor, Pasteur had the opportunity both to convalesce more completely and to test his theories about silkworm diseases. Napoleon III owned an estate in Trieste, in what is now northern Italy, that had harbored silkworms until they had been decimated by disease. The emperor proposed that Pasteur spend some time at the estate and attempt to reestablish silk-breeding there. Louis, Marie, and both children stayed at the Villa Vicentina from November 1869 through July 1870. Pasteur successfully supervised the establishment of healthy silkworms and finished his book on silkworm diseases, with his wife's constant help—he had come to rely on her assistance even more after his illness. The children learned Italian and read books about Napoleon I that Pasteur got for them from the library, in order to teach them lessons about "glory and devotion."

Away from Pasteur's disciplined regime, the silkworms did not always behave so well, nor did all the breeders appreciate his recommendations. With little experience or sympathy for life outside the laboratory, Pasteur was outraged when challenges and criticisms began to appear in newspapers and specialized agricultural journals. He responded to each and every one with indignation, sarcasm, and self-assurance. Even his illness supplied him with fighting material, as in this letter replying to one of his critics:

> Mr. Luppi speaks of my tone of confidence. Let him know at what price I acquired it. Let him know that I spent five years in tireless research, so unrelenting that it affected my health, probably permanently; but if my left side is paralyzed, my mind, thank God! has remained healthy enough to allow me to confound the detractors of my work and to ensure the triumph of truth.

Some of his critics were indeed careless or dishonest. Some failed to follow the recommendations exactly and then blamed Pasteur. Merchants who had been importing healthy Japanese silkworm eggs feared losing their business. For many, however, the threat came from the microscope.

Here was Pasteur, a scientist who waltzed down from Paris knowing nothing about silkworms, telling them to cast aside their traditional techniques and to search for invisible particles in silkworm guts. Those who could not afford microscopes, he suggested, could preserve the insects and send them to experts. No wonder there was resistance. In the developed world today, many farmers have academic degrees in agricultural science and readily turn to experts for advice, but the links between science and agriculture were just starting to be forged in the 19th century—by people such as Pasteur.

This was only one of several controversies in which Pasteur became embroiled during the 1860s and 1870s. He also responded to serious challenges to his work on pasteurization, fermentation, and spontaneous generation. Despite his stroke, he replied to each attack with gusto. He often brought these squabbles on himself. He would not rest until everyone agreed that his conclusions were correct, important, and original. Reluctant to recognize similarities between his work and that of others, he emphasized the novelty of his own, even if that required focusing on minor distinctions or quibbling over definitions. He claimed to approach nature with clear eyes, while his opponents were misled by preconceived ideas. His critics understandably bristled when he sent arrows down from on high, claiming that he hated to argue but had no choice but to defend Truth. He could not help it, he explained later in a letter to Ernest Legouvé, a playwright and a great-uncle to his son-in-law. He likened himself to a children's toy: When hearing someone make a stupid remark about his work, "I burst out of my shell like those devils closed up in a box that jump up armed from head to foot at the simple touch of a button."

Another controversy that occupied Pasteur in the 1860s, in addition to the struggle over silkworms, centered on the pasteurization of wine, for which he had taken out a patent. Alfred de Vergnette-Lamotte, a wealthy wine-producer and graduate of the École Polytechnique, challenged Pasteur's claim to have discovered the value of heating wine to preserve it from spoilage. After reading Pasteur's published articles, Vergnette-Lamotte, who had provided wine from his own vineyard for Pasteur's studies, complained that Pasteur had not sufficiently acknowledged either his contribution or that of Nicolas Appert, a food manufacturer who had invented canning, the method of preserving food by heating it in airtight containers. Pasteur replied that although others may have used heat as a preservative, they did not know why it worked; he had shown that heat killed the microorganisms that caused spoilage. The fight dragged on, with both having nasty letters published in agricultural journals, but Pasteur won, at least in the sense that people remember Pasteur, not Vergnette-Lamotte, as the inventor of the process named "pasteurization."

In the midst of these personal feuds, a fight on a much grander scale erupted. Just as the Pasteurs were returning from their sojourn in Trieste, the Franco-Prussian War began. Prussia, the strongest of the states that would soon combine to become Germany, launched a fierce attack on eastern France. The invading army advanced as far as Paris, where they besieged the city. The resulting famine was so severe that hungry Parisians ate dogs, cats, and even animals in the zoo. Napoleon III's empire fell, and a new government, the Third Republic, was formed in 1871.

Fearing that Paris was unsafe after they returned from Trieste in July 1870, Louis, Marie, and Marie-Louise soon fled to Pasteur's hometown of Arbois, where they stayed for several months. Meanwhile, Jean-Baptiste had enrolled in the army. Soon Arbois proved dangerous as well; the Pasteurs retreated south shortly before shots rang out in the vineyards and the Prussians occupied the town. The family searched for Jean-Baptiste among the bedraggled soldiers and found him safe and sound. Pasteur arranged for his transfer to duty in Switzerland. For three months the family stayed in Lyon with relatives, and then, from April to August 1871, in Clermont-Ferrand, where Émile Duclaux, one of Pasteur's students, was teaching.

The war did not curb Pasteur's ambition; in fact it had the opposite effect. Like bacteria thriving on decay, new projects and ideas bubbled up in his mind in the midst of the destruction. One element driving him was his intense patriotism. He viewed the Prussians as barbaric hordes, scoundrels and vandals, and hoped the war would extend through the winter so they would all die of cold and disease. "Every one of my works to my dying day will bear the epigraph: *Hatred to Prussia. Vengeance. Vengeance,*" he wrote to one of his students. He returned a diploma for an honorary degree that he had received from the University of Bonn, explaining that the document was now odious to him. Pasteur was also driven by his belief that France had lost the war because of a shameful lack of support for science teaching and research. Scientific laboratories in the German states were the most advanced in the world at the time, and many

Thousands of French soldiers were stationed in Paris as the German armies advanced in 1870. Many people, including Pasteur, felt bitterly humiliated when the city eventually surrendered, after a four-month siege.

commentators, not only Pasteur, connected this scientific superiority with Prussia's military might.

Incredibly, while in exile from occupied Paris, Pasteur continued to do research. In Lyon, he returned briefly to the wild experiments he had attempted years before, trying to create asymmetrical molecules by crystallizing different forms of racemic acid under the influence of an electromagnet. If he could succeed, he wrote to a former student, they would all have work for the rest of their lives and might find ways to make profound modifications of plants and animals. Soon, however, he turned back to more practical topics. He did more work on silkworms and then began a major study of beer.

The presence of a brewery in Clermont-Ferrand enabled Pasteur to carry out this study, in which he extended and solidified the research he had done on fermentation of wine and vinegar. Beer also appealed to his patriotism. France was not renowned for its beer, and Pasteur longed to change that reputation. Several years of assiduous study, including a trip to visit breweries in London, resulted in several patents, publication of *Studies on Beer* in 1876, and dreams that there would one day be a "Pasteur Beer." Pasteur

A certificate for a patent that Pasteur received for a new method of manufacturing beer.

characterized the different microorganisms that contaminated beer and proposed methods to keep the yeast pure and to hinder unwanted bacteria. Although French beer never soared to the heights that Pasteur envisioned, some large breweries adopted his techniques. The owner of the Carls-berg brewery in Denmark commissioned a marble bust of Pasteur in honor of his discoveries. His beer book was soon published in English, but Pasteur refused several requests to translate it into German, owing to his hostile feelings result-ing from the Franco-Prussian War.

Shortly after returning to Paris in fall of 1871, Pasteur requested early retirement from his position as chemistry professor at the Sorbonne, a job he had never fulfilled because of his illness and the war. He claimed that the gov-ernment owed him a pension for 30 years of university ser-vice (counting his student years) and because of his poor health. Two doctors and Jean-Baptiste Dumas signed state-ments declaring that Pasteur's intensive research on projects of national significance had led to his stroke. Pasteur explained that although he was too much of an invalid to teach, he would like to be appointed director of a laboratory at the École Normale (the emperor had formerly approved a new laboratory, on which construction had begun) and to be allowed to keep his apartment next to the laboratory. The president of the republic approved the request in 1874, and the National Assembly took the unusual step of award-ing him a lifetime salary of 12,000 francs per year, a com-fortable income, about what a lawyer or government official would earn.

With the promises of an expanded laboratory and a guaranteed salary, Pasteur could feel secure in his future. Like any parent, though, he still worried about his children. He and Marie were pleased when Jean-Baptiste married in 1874. Pasteur hoped that marriage would encourage his son to work harder. Jean-Baptiste had failed in his attempt to earn a law degree and had begun to study for the foreign service examination. Shortly after the wedding, Pasteur found out that Jean-Baptiste's mother-in-law was staying for long periods of time with the young couple. Little did she know that Pasteur's self-righteous wrath would fall on her. He wrote a letter accusing her of distracting Jean-Baptiste from his work and even claiming that her behavior threatened his own fragile health because it put him in a surly mood. Just as in his scientific debates, he allowed no room for compromise or debate: Any friend who read the letter, he wrote, would say "M[onsieur] Pasteur is absolutely right."

Pasteur's self-assurance may have been effective in his scientific work and in his personal relations, but it did not go far in the political realm. In 1875, he decided to run for a seat in the Senate. He presented himself as the candidate of conservatism, order, and law, promising, in a letter that appeared in three local publications, to replace the ineffective floundering of politics with the certainties of science:

> Science, in our century, is the soul of national prosperity, and the vital source of all progress. No doubt politics, with its tiresome, trivial debates, seems to be our guide. False appearances! What leads us is scientific discoveries and their applications.

Politics won and Pasteur lost—he received only 62 out of a total of 660 votes. Making the best of his defeat, he declared himself in a letter to his wife "very, very happy" not to have been elected.

Anyone watching the energy with which Pasteur took on new projects and defended old ones might have questioned his claim to be too sick to teach. No one seems to have minded, however; it was clear that Pasteur's genius thrived in the laboratory. Pasteur soon began intriguing and fruitful new projects on animal and human diseases, but at the same time he continued to vigilantly defend his previous work. In 1871 he responded handily to Liebig, who had recently published a long article challenging Pasteur's theory of fermentation. A much more disturbing challenge came in

1878, when Pasteur heard to his great surprise that an eminent colleague and—he thought—friend, Claude Bernard, had sabotaged him from the grave.

After Bernard's death, his friends found an unpublished manuscript detailing experiments he had recently undertaken to prove that fermentation could occur without the action of microorganisms. The army of devils popped up, and Pasteur counterattacked vigorously. He traveled to Arbois right away to set up experiments in his own vineyard; he called the scientist who had published Bernard's notes, Marcelin Berthelot, a scoundrel; he suggested that Bernard suffered both from poor sight and from interpretive blindness owing to preconceived ideas. It is just as well that he did not have access to other unpublished notes in which Bernard had accused Pasteur of the same fault: "Pasteur sees only what he's looking for. . . . [He] wants to direct nature; I let myself be directed by her." In only a few months, Pasteur had a lengthy, devastating reply ready for publication. He and Berthelot tussled back and forth for some time, but the issue was not finally resolved until a few years after Pasteur's death, when it became clear that there was truth to both Pasteur's and Bernard's views. Researchers discovered that certain types of molecules called "enzymes" inside cells can carry out the fermentation process even after the cells have been crushed and killed. Pasteur was right to call fermentation a process of living things; Bernard was right to maintain that it did not require the existence of living cells.

CHAPTER 5

"The Day the Sheep Died So Nicely"

What could a vat of fermenting wine or a hunk of ripe cheese possibly have in common with a sick person, delirious with fever and coughing up foul mucus? Fermentation and disease actually have many similarities, which were widely recognized before Pasteur began to explore them. Like fermentation, many diseases cause an increase in temperature; begin rapidly, peak, and then taper off; and produce frothy or slimy, sometimes evil-smelling products. Like contagious diseases, fermentation is "catching": A little vinegar added to wine will convert the whole batch to vinegar. And just as a fermented substance cannot ferment again (at least not in the same way), a person who has survived smallpox, measles, typhoid, or a number of other diseases, hardly ever gets the disease a second time.

From the early days of his work on fermentation, Pasteur had suggested that his results might eventually be useful for understanding and helping to prevent diseases in humans. In 1862, in a letter requesting government funds to enlarge his laboratory, Pasteur described his research as exploring the "mysterious phenomena of fermentation, phenomena so close to those of life, [and] even closer,

Sheep being vaccinated at Pouilly-le-Fort, where Pasteur staged a highly publicized test of a new vaccine against anthrax. In his report about this risky experiment, Pasteur made the often-quoted statement: "Chance favors the prepared mind."

perhaps, to those of death and disease, especially conta-gious diseases." For Pasteur, the secret to the mysteries of both fermentation and disease lay in the action of micro-scopic organisms, also called "microbes" (a term coined in 1878), or germs. We routinely live by the "germ theory of disease" today, as we scrub our kitchens with germ-killing cleansers and take antibiotics for infections, but when first developed this theory contradicted prevailing medical ideas, and so pitted the new breed of laboratory researchers against traditional physicians.

If not from germs, where did diseases come from? Most European physicians in the mid–19th century believed that diseases developed within the body from a combination of internal imbalances and unhealthy external conditions. The microorganisms that Pasteur kept touting as the cause of dis-ease seemed too small and too foreign to cause such pro-found physiological changes. These opponents of the germ theory contended that the causes of disease were inherited traits or personal habits such as alcoholism, or poor nutri-tion, and environmental conditions such as an unhealthy climate or dangerous "miasmas"—vapors from sewage, slaughterhouses, or swamps. Microorganisms simply flour-ished in the already unhealthy ground of the sick body. Many observations supported these theories. In fast-growing cities like Paris and London, for instance, death rates were higher among the poor, who lived in squalid conditions. And improved sanitation did work wonders. Florence Nightingale, an English nurse who reformed military hospitals during the Crimean War in the 1850s, did not believe in germs: In her view, her soldiers survived better when fed well and kept in clean and airy wards away from disease-causing miasmas.

Pasteur began his search for disease germs with an animal disease, anthrax, which was severely decimating livestock in Europe. Animals, usually sheep or cows, sickened and died suddenly, keeling over in pools of thick, dark blood. Bad air or some other environmental condition seemed to be the cause, especially since year after year the sickness returned to the same pastures. In the 1870s, however, several researchers isolated a microorganism from the blood of sick animals that they implicated as the cause. Casimir-Joseph Davaine, a physician who was familiar with Pasteur's work on fermenting microorganisms, found that he could give the disease to animals by injecting them with a small amount of a dead animal's blood that contained the rod-shaped bacteria. In 1876, a young German physician, Robert Koch, published a major paper on anthrax. Koch had discovered that when the anthrax bacteria were heated or dried out, they formed tiny spherical spores. The spores (bacteria in a dormant state, with a tough coat) could survive for a long time in harsh conditions; this seemed to explain why the disease persisted in certain locations.

Despite the work of Davaine and Koch, many veterinarians and physicians remained skeptical about the role of the microbe, and, indeed, experimental results were not clear-cut. One problem involved showing that the microbe rather than something in the blood caused the disease. Pasteur used an ingenious technique devised by Koch, called "successive dilutions." He placed a drop of bacteria-laden blood in a nutrient broth; then, when the bacteria had multiplied in the broth, placed a drop of that solution in a second flask of broth, and so on. The drop of blood became more and more dilute each time, but the bacteria continued to flourish. An injection with a solution that was full of bacteria but practically no blood killed an animal just as surely as an injection of blood.

Pasteur also explained how the disease could be transmitted to animals innocently grazing on soil above corpses buried several feet underground. Pasteur noticed, when walking in a pasture, that earthworms were busily burrowing in the soil. Could the worms be the germ carriers? He went to a site where animals dead of anthrax had been buried, collected worms, and injected the contents of their intestines into guinea pigs: The experimental animals soon came down with anthrax.

Clear proof of the cause and transmission of anthrax, yes? Well, no. Pasteur encountered resistance when he presented his results to the Academy of Medicine, to which he had been elected in 1873, especially from an elderly professor at a veterinary college, Gabriel Colin. Pasteur answered Colin's criticisms with biting sarcasm after presenting a paper at the Academy of Medicine in 1881. Referring to Colin's results, which contradicted his own, Pasteur scoffed, "If I take a clod of earth and find anthrax there, that's because it's there; and if, placing the same clod between the hands of M[onsieur] Colin, he doesn't find it, that's because he has made a mistake. One road leads to truth, a thousand to error. Colin always takes one of the latter."

The German scientist Robert Koch was one of the founders of bacteriology. The long-running feud between Koch and Pasteur was heightened by political conflicts between Germany and France.

Criticism also came from Koch, a fellow proponent of the germ theory. Koch believed that he himself had proven the anthrax bacterium to be the cause of the disease and claimed that Pasteur's studies added nothing new. He contested the earthworm theory—he could find no spores inside worms—and also criticized Pasteur's techniques for culturing (isolating and growing) bacteria, which were more prone to contamination than his own. Koch and Pasteur remained bitter rivals to the ends of their lives; ironically, they are remembered together today as cofounders of the germ theory. Koch is credited, in particular, as the father of bacteriology, the study of bacteria. He and other German researchers grouped bacteria into different types according to their ability to be stained by certain dyes and their shape (bacillus: rod-shaped; coccus: round; spirillum: spiral-shaped). The German bacteriologists also developed culture techniques that enabled them to isolate pure strains of bacteria.

Although challenges to his theories kept Pasteur busily on the defensive, he also basked in the praise of some prominent supporters, among them the English physician Joseph Lister. In 1874, Lister wrote to Pasteur to say that he had been inspired by Pasteur's discoveries about the role of germs in fermentation to develop an "antiseptic" method of surgery. By antiseptic, he meant using techniques intended to kill bacteria that might get into incisions, such as spraying carbolic acid during operations. Later, surgeons learned to use sterile, or "aseptic," methods to ban germs from the operating room altogether. Until the late 19th and early 20th centuries, surgery had been a dangerous treatment of last resort: As many as one in two patients died from post-operative infections.

Lister liked to take credit for reforming surgery, and Pasteur liked to take credit for inspiring Lister, but the story of surgery's progress does not jump quite so simply from great man to great man. Reduced mortality rates in hospitals came about not only through Lister's innovations but by a growing insistence on scrupulous cleanliness by surgeons and nurses—many of whom did not believe in the germ theory.

In 1879, an exciting family event distracted Pasteur's attention momentarily away from germs. Marie-Louise became engaged to René Vallery-Radot, secretary to the Minister of Public Works and a promising young author. Pasteur announced that he could find no flaws in his prospective son-in-law, despite a "microscopic" search, and was so excited he had trouble working (certainly a rare event). He particularly liked Vallery-Radot's patriotism and ambition. Although he never said so directly, Pasteur may have hoped that Vallery-Radot would make up for the dis-appointment he felt concerning his son, Jean-Baptiste. Pasteur feared that Jean-Baptiste and his wife were too

René Vallery-Radot, who married Pasteur's daughter Marie-Louise ("Zizi"), also charmed her parents. Madame Pasteur wrote to him, "I am so fond of you, and you know so well how to be amiable, that I have no qualms at the thought of entrusting dear little Zizi to your care."

attached to life's pleasures, and he constantly nagged "J.-B." to work harder. He even urged him to go on a diet, so that he would be as trim as Vallery-Radot (who kept fit through stints in the army reserves).

Vallery-Radot proved to be the perfect son-in-law. He not only provided the Pasteurs with grandchildren, something J.-B. had failed to do, but helped to make a hero of his father-in-law by writing his biography. The first version, published anonymously in 1884 and carefully checked by Pasteur, was called *Histoire d'un Savant par un Ignorant* (History of a Scientist by a Layman). A fuller version, published in 1900, after Pasteur's death, remained the standard biography of Pasteur for decades. It painted him as a benevolent genius and quietly bypassed his less attractive features. Later, René and Marie-Louise's son, Louis Pasteur Vallery-Radot, collected and published four volumes of his grandfather's correspondence and seven volumes of his written works.

The letters of Pasteur and his wife at this time, when their children married and left home, reveal something of their own relationship, which had by now settled into a comfortable routine. In a letter to Vallery-Radot, Marie assured him that Marie-Louise "will have no thoughts other than yours; she will interest herself in your work and your success, as she has seen me always doing in the case of her good father." Later, when they were in Arbois during their yearly summer "vacation," she wrote to her daughter that she kept busy all day recopying her husband's articles for publication, and that she could barely entice him to take a walk.

Pasteur appreciated his wife's devotion: As he explained to his children, "the wife makes the husband. Every prosperous household is served by a good-hearted, energetic woman." But he could be testy, too. Writing to Marie in Paris after he had gone to Arbois to do some experiments, he complained that one of his shirts was missing a button, that another was torn, and a third had a button sewn on too tightly. "Oh! Women!" he scolded, "How little you know what your husbands need." The Pasteurs divided up tasks in a way that was typical for middle-class couples in 19th-century France: The husband pursued work in the public world, while the wife had responsibility for the home and children. Pasteur exercised his authority more strongly than some men, however. When a colleague, Monsieur Guillaume-Jules Houel, turned down a job because his wife did not want to move away from her family, Pasteur wrote to express his incredulity: He could not believe that Madame Houel would sacrifice her husband's career to satisfy her own sentimental feelings.

Back in the laboratory after his daughter's marriage, Pasteur began to explore a new approach to disease: prevention by induced immunity. Everyone knew that once you had certain diseases you were then immune—that is, you would not get them again. Until the end of the 19th century, however, only one disease, smallpox, was widely controlled by deliberately making people immune to it. Many societies throughout the world had developed techniques for protecting people from this disfiguring and often fatal disease. In Africa, for instance, local healers would scratch a healthy person's skin, then rub in some of the pus from a sore of a person with a mild case of smallpox. Occasionally, inoculated people became very sick or died, but most of the time they developed only a slight illness and were thereafter resistant to the disease. In the 1720s, this technique was introduced from Turkey to England and spread throughout Europe. The method was substantially improved by Edward Jenner, an English physician, in the 1790s. He discovered that if people were inoculated with cowpox, a related disease, instead of smallpox, they became immune to smallpox while avoiding the risk of developing a severe illness. This immunization procedure was called "vaccination," from the Latin word *vacca,* or cow.

Would a similar technique work for other diseases? Although some attempts were made, it was not until the 1880s that researchers developed new types of "vaccines." The first major breakthrough came from Pasteur's laboratory, with vaccinations against chicken cholera and anthrax. (Pasteur borrowed the word "vaccination," which had been used only for smallpox, and since then it has been used for immunizing inoculations against any disease.) The circumstances around the development of these vaccines are not completely clear, and historians have only recently uncovered some of the details of how they were prepared and who prepared them. Pasteur never liked describing the dead ends and false starts of laboratory work, and he was particularly reluctant to reveal any clues that would give an advantage to his rivals. Like most heads of laboratories at the time, he also tended to take credit himself for ideas and work actually done by his co-workers and assistants.

Pasteur and his team began their study of chicken cholera by isolating the bacterium that caused the disease and keeping it alive in the laboratory in flasks of chicken broth. One day, they injected material from an old culture (bacteria-filled broth) into some chickens, which remained healthy. Because injections from a new culture would have killed the chickens, it seemed as though the chicken cholera bacteria had become weakened, or attenuated. Now came the really important finding: When material from a fresh young culture was injected into chickens that had first been inoculated with the old culture, the chickens remained healthy. Uninoculated chickens injected with the young culture died. These results showed that it was possible to prevent chickens from contracting chicken cholera—the germ had been disarmed.

Pasteur claimed, and, until recently, his biographers have repeated, that he made this discovery himself through a combination of luck (mistakenly allowing the cultures to age) and genius (coming up with the idea of testing the injected chickens for immunity). According to historians who have examined Pasteur's laboratory notebooks, though, the discovery was largely the work of a deliberate investigation undertaken by his assistant, Émile Roux .

During his later years, Pasteur relied heavily—for both labor and ideas—on a first-rate team that included Roux, Charles Chamberland, Louis Thuillier, and Émile Duclaux. Many of them went on to distinguished careers of their own. Although loyal and devoted to Pasteur, Roux, more than the others, pursued his own ideas, and the two men skirmished now and then. Roux was a medical student when he first started working in Pasteur's laboratory in 1878, and he contributed essential elements that Pasteur lacked: expertise and legitimacy in medicine. A tall, thin man with eyes like deep wells and a quick temper, he was more austere than Pasteur but shared his mentor's intensity and stubbornness. After he contracted tuberculosis in the 1880s, Roux kept the disease at bay for decades by paying close attention to his diet and lying in bed for exactly 12 hours a day.

Even if he no longer worked alone, Pasteur was the one in the line of fire, taking both credit and criticism. He wrangled particularly with physicians, who did not appreciate a chemist invading their territory, especially one as arrogantly sarcastic as Pasteur. When he first began working on contagious diseases, Pasteur frequently acknowledged that he was ignorant of medical matters. But if someone else accused him of ignorance, that was a different matter. Long-simmering resentments boiled over in

The physician Émile Roux preferred working in the laboratory to treating patients. A devoted disciple of Pasteur, he was head of the Pasteur Institute from 1904 to 1933.

late 1880, when Pasteur almost came to blows after a debate in the Academy of Medicine about vaccination. That summer he had announced the successful preparation of a vaccine against chicken cholera but refused to give details. His reticence angered, among others, Jules Guérin, an 80-year-old surgeon who did not believe that Pasteur's invisible germs caused disease. One afternoon, after a particularly intense battle of insults, Guérin threw himself at Pasteur and had to be pulled away. The next day Guérin challenged Pasteur to a duel. Negotiations were carried on via the president of the Academy, who kept the two scientists from facing off with pistols.

Pasteur knew that convincing his opponents would require a dramatic demonstration, and he supplied one the following spring during a public trial of the anthrax vaccine. It was a close call, though, that could easily have turned out badly. Preparing the anthrax vaccine had been much trickier than Pasteur expected. He had confidently declared in a published paper that anthrax bacteria could be attenuated (made less virulent) by the same method as that used for chicken cholera—exposure to oxygen—and had hinted that an anthrax vaccine was in the works. In the laboratory, though, the oxygen-attenuation method was not producing good results.

In 1881, one of Pasteur's critics called him on his boast that he could produce an anthrax vaccine. Hippolyte Rossignol, a veterinary surgeon who had ridiculed Pasteur and his belief in microorganisms, offered a challenge on behalf of a local agricultural society: The society would provide Pasteur with several dozen animals to use for a large-scale, public trial of the vaccine at Rossignol's farm, Pouilly-le-Fort. Pasteur accepted. He immediately summoned Roux and Chamberland, who were on vacation, back to the lab, and everyone went into high gear—they knew that they did not yet have a reliable vaccine and feared disaster if the experiment failed.

Pasteur continued attempts at oxygen attenuation, still with unreliable results. In the meantime, Roux had discovered that Jean-Joseph Toussaint, a professor at the Toulouse Veterinary School who was also working on a vaccine, was experimenting with a new technique, attenuating the bacteria using antiseptic compounds such as carbolic acid. Chamberland and Roux tried out the antiseptic attenuation method, and it worked. May 5 arrived, the day for the first injection of vaccine into 24 sheep, 6 cows, and 1 goat at Pouilly-le-Fort. Pasteur had no choice but to use the reliable vaccine prepared by his assistants, using Toussaint's method, rather than his own. On May 17, the animals received a second vaccination, of a slightly stronger strain. May 31 was the point of no return: the vaccinated animals, along with an unvaccinated group of 24 sheep, 4 cows, and 1 goat, received injections of a killing solution of anthrax germs. The experiment had been widely publicized. A crowd of 150 gathered for the final injection, and even more were expected to arrive on June 2 to see which animals had become sick or died. Pasteur, Roux, and Chamberland returned to Paris to wait with suspense for the outcome.

On June 1, word arrived that some of the vaccinated sheep were sick, and it looked as though the experiment might fail. Pasteur threw a fit, accusing Roux of carelessness and telling him he would have to go to Pouilly-le-Fort by himself, to face the crowd alone. The morning of the big day, Pasteur changed his mind after receiving a reassuring telegram. Pasteur, Roux, and Chamberland arrived at Pouilly-le-Fort to a cheering crowd, which included several politicians and a reporter for the *Times* of London. The results of the experiment were there for all to see, in the stark contrast of life versus death. All the vaccinated animals appeared healthy; all but two of the unvaccinated sheep and the goat were dead. The remaining two cooperated by dying for the audience. The unvaccinated cows, which were

Pasteur became a public figure after his laboratory developed an anthrax vaccine. Caricatures in newspapers and popular magazines showed him with the animals his treatments had saved.

known to be more resistant to the disease, were still alive, but had large swellings and fever. Pasteur was jubilant. "Oh ye of little faith," he chided those in the gathered crowd who had doubted him and accepted the new believers in the germ theory as "converted sinners."

This dramatic and highly publicized success, which was widely reported in newspapers, did much to promote the germ theory. A few of Pasteur's critics, including Koch, discredited the results, and a test of the vaccine in Italy failed miserably. But other trials around France and abroad confirmed the vaccine's effectiveness. Requests for vaccine poured in, and Chamberland set up a facility for producing it in quantity. By 1894, little more than a decade after Pouilly-le-Fort, 3,400,000 sheep had been vaccinated. France recognized Pasteur by awarding him the Grand Cross, the highest rank in the Legion of Honor, and, the next year, raising the amount of his national salary from 12,000 to 25,000 francs per year. At Pasteur's request, Roux and Chamberland were made *chevaliers* (knights) in the legion.

The Pasteur family received more good news the day of the success at Pouilly-le-Fort. In a letter to her daughter, Madame Pasteur wrote, "The day when our 25 sheep died so nicely, we also learned of the death of M[onsieur] Littré." Madame Pasteur did not usually rejoice at someone's death; but this case was significant because it opened up a seat in the Académie Française. The Académie, the most prestigious scholarly institution in France, was limited to 40 men (no woman was elected until 1980). The members, who were referred to as "immortals," were supposed to defend the purity of the French language (the Académie published an influential dictionary), and most of them were literary figures. Important people in other fields sometimes gained admission, though. As the most prominent scientist in the country, Pasteur had a good chance of being elected. Madame Pasteur was so confident, in fact, that she immediately started clipping obituaries of Littré from newspapers. If elected, Pasteur would have to give a speech praising his predecessor.

Pasteur and his friends lined up supporters, and in December 1881 he learned that he had been elected. He agonized over his speech, since he disliked Littré's liberal politics and lack of religious conviction. In the end, standing in the Académie's ornate chamber on April 27, 1882, clad in a green-and-gold frock coat, he frankly stated his disagreement with Littré's ideas and delivered a rousing defense of religious sentiment, after accepting the honor not for himself, but for science. "His features are strongly marked, his eyes are lively, his body is robust," reported a journalist. "His masculine and clipped speech reveals a man for whom there is neither obstacle nor fatigue." The Académie director then welcomed him, explaining that the immortals had recognized in him the spark of genius that inspires great work in all fields. "No one has walked with such a sure step on the paths of elementary nature; your scientific work is like a luminous ray in the vast night of the infinitely small, in those utmost depths of being where life is born. . . . Take your place with the elite who assure themselves against nothingness by a single method: creating works that last."

Pasteur always kept careful notes of his experiments. The paralyzed rabbit sketched here had been injected with saliva from another rabbit, which had been infected by a rabid dog.

CHAPTER 6

"My Hand Will Tremble When I Go On to Man"

"While Pasteur may have been celebrated in the Geneva Congress as a second Jenner, the celebration was somewhat premature," sniped Pasteur's rival, Robert Koch, in 1882. "In the surge of enthusiasm, one forgot that Jenner's discovery [of the smallpox vaccine] had value for humans rather than for sheep." The barb hit a sensitive spot. Although his election to the Académie Française had certified Pasteur as the leading scientist in France, he had not yet realized his dream of applying his work on microorganisms to human disease. Koch, by contrast, had already begun to tackle tuberculosis, the most deadly contagious disease in Europe. His announcement in 1882 that he had discovered the tuberculosis microbe had been heralded with excitement and raised hopes for a cure.

Pasteur did have projects underway on several other diseases besides anthrax. One of them was a disease of pigs, swine erysipelis, for which he had developed a vaccine, but he had also begun tentative explorations of human illnesses.

Hoping to discover the yellow fever microbe, he charged to Bordeaux in 1881 when he heard that passengers on ships arriving from Senegal, where an epidemic was raging, were dying like flies. According to Madame Pasteur, he departed as though going off to war. His desire to battle microbes was frustrated, however. First the ships were delayed, then they arrived with no dead or dying passengers: The corpses had already been thrown overboard. Not one to waste time, he spent several productive weeks in the library working on the speech he would deliver when inducted into the Académie Française.

In early 1883, cholera swept into Egypt, which had been invaded and occupied by the British the previous year. Before it was over, tens of thousands of people had succumbed to the disease, which kills quickly by dehydration (water loss) resulting from uncontrollable diarrhea. This time instead of going himself, Pasteur obtained government permission to send a team: Émile Roux, his physician colleague; Isidore Straus, also a physician; Edmond Nocard, a professor from a veterinary school; and Louis Thuillier, an energetic young assistant in Pasteur's laboratory. A week after the French team arrived in the Egyptian port city Alexandria, Robert Koch showed up with a competing German team. The opposing camps examined blood, diarrhea, vomit, and tissues from dead bodies, and fed or injected material from cholera victims to mice, cats, dogs, monkeys, and chickens. The French team reported disappointing results. The microscope revealed hosts of bacteria, but it was impossible to tell which might be the culprit, since no animals exposed to suspect germs became ill. The epidemic soon subsided, and, along with it, experimental material. Then, one night, Thuillier woke up feeling sick. A little more than 24 hours later he died, despite being treated with opium, ether injections, and chilled champagne. His death was one of the last in the epidemic.

Pasteur, distressed by the tragedy, did what he could—he arranged for a street to be named after Thuillier and found a job for his brother—but, as he wrote to a colleague, "What good does all that do now?" Thuillier's death was not the only bad news to arrive from Egypt. In addition, it looked as though the German team was winning the race to find the cholera microbe. Koch, who was more experienced than his French rivals in identifying bacteria, announced that he had found a distinctive comma-shaped microbe that existed only in the intestines of cholera patients. From Egypt he went to India, where the disease was common, and confirmed his observation after dozens of autopsies.

Pasteur never got over the sting of France's defeat in the Franco-Prussian War, and he hated seeing German scientists celebrated for discovering the cause of cholera. When an epidemic struck the French city of Toulon in 1884, he sent Roux and Isidore Straus to investigate. To the annoyance of the French team, Koch arrived too. Pasteur instructed Roux to try to find some mistake in Koch's work. Do not by any means do autopsies together, he urged in a letter: "Keep your corpses to yourselves." Apparently Roux and Straus disobeyed, for in his published paper on cholera Koch described smugly how he had had to point out the cholera microbes to Roux and Straus when the three men had autopsied a sailor together.

If Pasteur had not gotten far on yellow fever and cholera, he had high hopes for rabies, which he had begun to work on in late 1880. This project, Pasteur's last major undertaking, brought together all his talents and resources: dogged persistence, ingenious creativity, generous government support, superb assistants, adept self-promotion, and just plain luck. He went at it with his usual focused intensity. "Your father is absorbed in his thoughts," wrote Madame Pasteur in a letter to Marie-Louise in 1884. "[He] talks little, sleeps little, rises at dawn, and in one word continues the life I began with him this day 35 years ago."

Why rabies? Although it was an insignificant source of mortality, killing only a few dozen people in France per

Pasteur in his laboratory at the École Normale Supérieure in 1885. "If there were no laboratories, the physical sciences would become the image of sterility and death," wrote Pasteur.

year, in contrast to the tens of thousands felled by tuberculosis, diphtheria, typhoid, and cholera, its gruesome horrors riveted people's attention in the same way that stories of plane crashes do today. It was a horrible way to die. First, the attack by an enraged animal, followed by cauterization of the wound (searing with a caustic agent such as acid or red-hot metal). Then the long wait of months or even a year to see if the "virus," or "poison," had taken hold. Once the disease appeared, death followed like night after day. Doctors and family members could only watch helplessly as the doomed victim suffered headaches, convulsions, and delirium. A cure for rabies would have a great effect on the public imagination, if not on public health. Another advantage of rabies was that, unlike cholera or yellow fever, it afflicted both animals and people and so offered a perfect transition from veterinary to human medicine.

As he had done for other diseases, Pasteur first tried to find a rabies microbe. Amazingly, he decided to continue work on the disease even though he never succeeded. If rabies could not be cultured in laboratory flasks, it would just have to be cultured in animal bodies instead. In fact, neither Pasteur nor anyone else in the 19th century could have seen the agent that causes rabies since it is not a bacterium but a virus, a particle on the borderline between living and nonliving matter so small that several million could fit on a one-inch line. The viruses responsible for rabies, smallpox, influenza, and many other nonbacterial diseases were not detectable until the invention of high-powered electron microscopes in the 1930s. In the 19th century, people used the term "virus" very broadly, to mean any poison or particle that transmitted disease.

Other obstacles, besides the elusiveness of the rabies microbe, had to be overcome. To study rabies in the laboratory, Pasteur and his assistants had to find a reliable way to transmit the disease from one animal to another, and they also needed to shorten the time it took for an animal to become sick, which could take several months. Roux, knowing that the disease primarily affected nerves, wondered if it would be possible to directly infect the largest nerve center in the body, the brain. He anesthetized a dog, cut a small hole in its skull, and put some infected nerve tissue on its brain. The method, called "trephination," worked. Dogs treated in this way always contracted rabies and usually died within two weeks.

The team now began to search for a technique to produce a vaccine. They had not isolated any rabies microorganism, and they did not know how animals became immune to diseases. They had lots of animals and laboratory help, though, and so they tried everything they could think of. They injected dogs with saliva, blood, or ground-up brains of rabid rabbits. They tried different preparations of these materials in different amounts. They investigated "serial passage," passing the disease from animal to animal up to 90 times in guinea pigs, rabbits, and monkeys. Most of these experiments were never published; historians have reconstructed them from Pasteur's laboratory notebooks. In his published work, Pasteur, like many researchers, led his readers along a direct, well-cleared trail, and did not describe his exploratory forays into the chaotic forest of possibilities.

When he was ready to go public, Pasteur announced some exciting results to the Academy of Sciences in February and May 1884 and in an address to a medical congress in Copenhagen in August of that year. Pasteur described the technique of serial passage and explained that in rabbits and guinea pigs, the virus became more virulent as it passed from animal to animal until about the 25th, when the effect leveled off. At this point, a rabbit would die six to eight days after inoculation. In monkeys, however, the opposite occurred. Each monkey took longer to become ill. Monkeys, then, could be used to produce an attenuated, or weakened, virus, just what was needed for a vaccine. In the Copenhagen address, Pasteur declared that he had produced such a vaccine and had rendered 23 dogs immune to rabies.

Pasteur then threw out a tantalizing suggestion. If dogs could be made immune, could not humans? The time between becoming infected and developing symptoms (the incubation period) is unusually long in the case of rabies—from one month up to, in rare cases, one year. Perhaps humans could be vaccinated and thus made immune after they had been bitten, but before the virus had taken hold?

The prospect of a rabies cure attracted public attention, but not all the attention was positive. A small but vocal group objected strenuously to Pasteur's animal experiments. It was no secret that hundreds of animals died miserably in his laboratories in Paris and at Villeneuve l'Étang, just west of the city, where a kennel for 60 dogs had been constructed on the site of a former royal palace. Rabid dogs barked themselves hoarse and tore at the bars of their cages; guinea pigs and rabbits convulsed to death more quietly. Even Madame Pasteur, who was used to her husband's experiments, was moved by a scene that she described to her daughter: "Yesterday we watched a poor monkey die 48 hours after it had been inoculated with anthrax. Its companion, vaccinated against the same illness, would not let go of the wretched corpse even though M.[onsieur] Roux was hitting it with a switch. Finally they subdued it by wrapping it up in a net."

To antivivisectionists, foes of experiments on live animals, Pasteur was a murderer. During the late 19th century, organized movements grew up in England, France, and the United States to protest vivisection—cutting or other painful procedures performed on living animals. Antivivisectionists put forth several arguments against animal experimentation. They challenged the scientific benefit, claiming that results from animals could not be applied to

This engraving, "Vivisection—The Last Appeal," was circulated in England in the mid-1880s. The image of the winsome dog begging for mercy was clearly intended to evoke outrage at scientists' experiments on animals.

humans, and that a mutilated body could not supply useful information about normal function anyway. On ethical grounds, they argued that it was immoral for humans to abuse innocent animals. They also contended that cruelty to animals inevitably led to a lack of feeling for fellow human beings. Defenders of the practice responded that the sacrifice of a few animals was necessary for medical advances that would benefit both humans and other animals in the long run. To that argument, the British antivivisectionist Lord Coleridge replied, "If it could be proved that anybody's life had been prolonged by these practices, our answer is, that if the vivisectors could make us all live to be a hundred it would be a miserable extinction of pity in the human heart. It is comparatively unimportant how long we live; what matters is how we live."

In England, the movement bore fruit in the Cruelty to Animals Act, passed in 1876, which required scientists to obtain permits for certain types of animal experimentation. Although the act was quite moderate (too much so for some activists), scientists did not like this government intrusion into their laboratories. Delegates to the 1881 International Medical Congress in London—attended by both Pasteur and Koch—unanimously passed a general resolution stating that experiments on animals are useful and necessary and should not be regulated, although scientists should attempt to avoid inflicting undue pain.

Pasteur was a favorite target for English activists. One of the most prominent, Anna Kingsford, who had received a medical degree in Paris, believed she had occult powers that enabled her to kill vivisectors like Pasteur by means of mental energy. Several antivivisection societies were also founded in France, but the movement attracted fewer followers than in England, and Pasteur was able to continue his experiments without any hindrance (other than Kingsford's ineffective mental rays). In moving on to develop a rabies

text continued on page 94

WHEN THE GUINEA PIGS ARE HUMAN

Studying contagious diseases in animals posed no ethical problems to most 19th-century researchers. Humans, though, were a different story. "The great difficulty in the study of contagious diseases in the human species lies in the impossibility of doing experiments on people," noted Pasteur. Physicians in western Europe traditionally swore to uphold the Hippocratic Oath, a set of doctrines formulated in ancient Greece, which includes the mandate that the physician should "do no harm." Self-interest also urged caution. Scientists knew that a few failures could turn public sentiment against them.

How, then, was the physician to try out a new remedy or test a theory? Like Pasteur, many scientists first tried experiments on animals. But humans sometimes react differently than animals, and some human diseases cannot be induced in animals. Researchers have developed several methods for making the leap from animals to humans.

One way to test a theory without endangering people is to perform a natural experiment—to compare groups of people who have been exposed naturally to different conditions. Koch did just this when he was studying cholera. He wanted to know if the bacterium he had discovered actually caused the disease, but he could not find any susceptible animals. He could not ethically give cholera bacteria to a person. He discovered, however, that the sheets and clothes of cholera patients were full of the suspected bacteria, and that in India the people who washed these linens often got the disease. This suggested, but did not prove, that the bacterium caused the disease.

Another strategy scientists used was to experiment on themselves, their families, or colleagues. One of the most infamous episodes occurred in 1892, when Max von Pettenkofer, a critic of Koch's theories, swallowed a cholera cocktail: bouillon laced with millions of cholera microbes. All he got was a mild case of diarrhea (thus showing that exposure alone does not necessarily lead to disease). Pasteur, too, considered self-experimentation. He wrote to a friend that he was tempted to give himself rabies and then treat himself with the vaccine. He resisted the temptation, however.

Before he considered trying the vaccine on himself, Pasteur had another idea: What about criminals condemned to death? Until quite recently, many researchers considered it ethical to experiment on people who were either about to die anyway or who could not say "no" for one reason or another: prisoners, military personnel, slaves, orphans, mentally retarded people, uneducated people, or patients confined in hospitals. Pasteur wrote to the emperor of Brazil asking him to consider giving prisoners condemned to die the option of being injected with experimental rabies vaccine. "If the . . . convict agreed to these trials, his life would be spared." The emperor responded that because capital punishment had been indefinitely suspended in Brazil, he did not think any prisoners would agree to risk a potentially lethal inoculation.

Finally, an experimental treatment might be tried out on a few willing subjects and then, if successful, applied more broadly. Edward Jenner used this method when he inoculated a young boy with cowpox and then later with smallpox, to see if he had become immune to smallpox. The trouble with this method is that conclusions about how safe and effective a treatment will be when given to thousands or millions of people cannot be made from the results on one or two.

Since the 19th century, standards of human experimentation have transformed because of changes in scientific method and ethical standards as well as publicity surrounding some notorious cases of carelessness and abuse. In the 20th century, national and international organizations formulated codes and regulations concerning human experimentation. These include the 1948 Nuremberg Code, adopted after World War II; the Declaration of Helsinki, drafted by the World Medical Association in 1964; and regulations adopted by individual countries. All these codes insist on informed consent: The subject must understand the risks involved and choose freely whether or not to participate.

The testing of new drugs and vaccines now is much more extensive, scientific, and bureaucratic than it was in Pasteur's day. In the 1960s, the U.S. government began to establish guidelines for testing on human subjects. Regulations instituted by the National Research Act of 1974 and updated in

A romanticized portrayal of Edward Jenner inoculating a child with cowpox, to provide immunity against small-pox. Jenner's first experimental subjects were neighbors and family members.

1981 set out detailed procedures for clinical trials of new medical treatments. Testing often takes several years and occurs in three phases, each of which involves larger numbers of people. It all sounds good on paper, but complications inevitably arise. AIDS (acquired immunodeficiency syndrome) has raised particularly difficult problems because of its deadliness and long incubation time. Should a potentially beneficial drug be released before studies are completed? How can the efficacy of a vaccine be judged if it may take years for people to develop the disease after they are exposed to HIV (human immunodeficiency virus)? Is it ethical for researchers in the developed world to conduct clinical trials in third–world countries?

No codes can completely do away with the ethical dilemmas that human experimentation raises, or the potent temptations of curiosity and glory that sometimes entice scientists to forget that people are not guinea pigs.

text continued from page 90

vaccine for humans, however, Pasteur faced ethical obstacles that he could not ignore. He could not simply subject groups of people to different treatments and see how many died, as he could with animals.

Pasteur hoped to develop a fail-safe vaccine for dogs and then, in cooperation with a physician, to try it out in humans. The ethical dilemmas might seem slight, since rabies is fatal and the vaccine would be given only after a person was exposed to the disease. If the vaccine worked, the victim would be saved from an agonizing death. If it did not, or if it caused complications, even fatal ones, well, the person would have died anyway. Unfortunately, things were not so simple. Many animals that bit people did not have rabies, and most people bitten by animals that were rabid never came down with the disease. Death was certain only after symptoms appeared, and by that time, a vaccine might come too late. And the vaccine might not work the same way in people as it did in dogs. No wonder Pasteur felt, as he stated in a letter to Pedro III, emperor of Brazil, that "my hand will tremble when I go on to man."

Before jumping the divide to humans, a better vaccine was needed. The technique of attenuating, or weakening, the virus by passing it through monkeys turned out to be less reliable than Pasteur had claimed, and it was also a very slow procedure. Pasteur discovered a new method by peeking into Émile Roux's incubation room. Roux and Pasteur were both working on rabies, but somewhat independently. One day Pasteur was helping his nephew Adrien Loir, who worked in the laboratory, carry materials to an incubator that Roux used for his experiments. According to Loir, Pasteur suddenly picked up a flask on Roux's shelf, examined it keenly, and left without saying a word. That afternoon, Roux discovered three similar flasks in Pasteur's workroom. When Loir explained that Pasteur had prepared these flasks after having seen Roux's flask, Roux stalked angrily out of the building. "From this moment on," wrote

Loir, "rabies became a dead letter for Roux; he stopped working on it and no longer came to the laboratory during the day."

When Pasteur had looked at Roux's flask, he had seen a rabbit's spinal cord dangling by a string from a cotton plug in the top, and a lump of potash in the bottom. What was so exciting about that? Pasteur realized that Roux had discovered a way to weaken a strong form of the rabies virus present in the spinal cord by drying it in air. From then on he took the technique as his own, and, after considerable trial and error, found a way to make a more reliable vaccine. The technique worked like this: Every day, one of Pasteur's assistants would remove the spinal cords from laboratory rabbits that had just died from rabies and hang them in flasks to dry. Pieces of the cord would be snipped out and mixed with sterile broth. A dog would first be injected with a solution containing mashed-up spinal cord tissue that had dried for 14 days and was too weak to make the dog sick. Each day, the dog would be injected with spinal cord that was one day fresher. The last injection, of one-day-old cord, would have killed a dog that had not received the earlier injections.

As Pasteur was developing his vaccine, he kept wondering if the time had come to try it in humans. It was widely known that he was working on rabies, and people often contacted him for help. To a request that arrived at the end of 1884, he wrote in reply, "I dare not try anything yet on humans." Soon, he did dare. Then, as now, people disagreed about whether he took too great a risk when he first tried

The spinal cord of a rabid rabbit hangs inside a flask. Pasteur and his colleagues were able to develop a vaccine after discovering that the rabies virus gradually diminished in strength as the spinal cord dried.

the vaccine on people. Roux seems to have felt so, for he apparently refused to participate in the first few trials. As he had done in his other work, Pasteur worked quietly until he could announce a success. Then, in a scientific paper presented in October 1885, he broadcast the great news that his rabies vaccine had saved two young boys, Joseph Meister and Jean-Baptiste Jupille, from certain death.

In fact, the first two people Pasteur treated with rabies vaccine were not Meister and Jupille, but a 61-year-old man named Girard and an 11-year-old girl, Julie-Antoinette Poughon, in May and June 1885. Both had been bitten by dogs and were already exhibiting symptoms of what might be rabies when the doctors who examined them called on Pasteur. Girard received one injection of vaccine, but the hospital authorities decided not to allow any more. He seemed to improve and was released from the hospital, but his fate is unknown. Poughon received two shots but died shortly after the second. Presumably the disease was too far advanced by the time she received the vaccine (she had been bitten more than a month before the treatment). Beyond a very small circle, no one knew about these patients until historians found Pasteur's notes about them in his laboratory papers.

The next opportunity to try out the vaccine came just two weeks after Poughon's death, on July 6, 1885. Three people came directly to Pasteur's laboratory from Alsace: a nine-year-old boy, Joseph Meister, who had been badly bitten on the hand and legs; his mother; and the dog's owner, a grocer who had shot and killed the dog after it had nipped him. The boy seemed to be in danger because the dog had sunk its teeth deep into his flesh. Pasteur consulted with two physicians and finally decided to treat Meister. He had a room prepared for the boy and his mother, not in a hospital but in an annex to one of his laboratories. The first injection was given on the evening of July 6, two days after the boy had been attacked. Pasteur's colleague Dr. Joseph Grancher pulled up a fold of skin on Meister's abdomen and emptied a syringe full of mashed-up spinal cord from a rabbit that had died of rabies on June 21, 14 days before the injection. Pasteur looked on: Because he was not a physician, he could not administer the injection himself. Each day, for 11 days, Grancher gave the boy an injection of ever-stronger rabies virus. On the last day, the injection contained material from the spinal cord of a rabbit that had died the day before. In an uninoculated person, this injection would be fatal, and in later cases Pasteur rarely went so far. Resistance to this final inoculation, however, would indicate that the earlier ones had conferred immunity.

The decision to treat Joseph Meister was much riskier than those involving the two previous patients. The first two had already developed symptoms; Meister had none, and it was not absolutely certain either that the dog was rabid or that Meister would get the disease. If Meister was going to get rabies, and the vaccine worked, Pasteur would have saved his life. On the other hand, if Meister had not contracted the disease and the vaccine turned out to be too strong, then the treatment itself might kill him. Pasteur had just barely begun to test this new vaccine in dogs. Not until late May of 1885 had he tried the "Meister technique" (injections of progressively more and more virulent spinal cord) on dogs. By July, when the boy arrived at his laboratory, experiments were under way on 40 dogs, but half of them had been injected in late June, too recently to tell if they would become ill. Unlike Meister, none of these dogs had been exposed to rabies before being treated.

On the day before Meister was to receive the last injection, Madame Pasteur wrote to her daughter and son-in-law, "this will be another bad night for your father. He cannot come to terms with the idea of applying a measure of last resort to this child [the final, virulent, inoculation]. And yet he now has to go through with it." Meister remained healthy, and Pasteur breathed a sigh of relief and pride.

Jean-Baptiste Jupille is injected with rabies vaccine by Dr. Grancher, while Pasteur looks on. The story of the heroic shepherd was widely publicized.

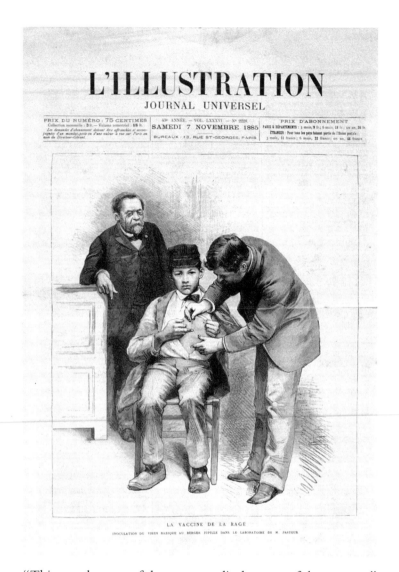

L'ILLUSTRATION
JOURNAL UNIVERSEL

PRIX DU NUMÉRO : 75 CENTIMES · 43ᵉ ANNÉE — VOL. LXXXVI — Nº 2228 · PRIX D'ABONNEMENT

SAMEDI 7 NOVEMBRE 1885

BUREAUX : 13, RUE ST-GEORGES, PARIS.

LA VACCINE DE LA RAGE
INOCULATION DU VIRUS RABIQUE AU BERGER JUPILLE DANS LE LABORATOIRE DE M. PASTEUR

"This may be one of the great medical events of the century," he predicted to his son-in-law, René. Shortly after the treatment had been completed, he and Madame Pasteur left for Arbois. He made Meister promise to write to him every day. Not only did it look as though the vaccine had succeeded, but Pasteur had pulled a patriotic coup, as well. Meister was from Alsace, a province that the Germans had snatched from France during the Franco-Prussian War, and which they still occupied. "I am so happy that this success is a French one,"

Pasteur wrote to a colleague, "and that the first human subject in whom rabies has been halted after a bite is from Alsace."

The news about Meister leaked out, and Pasteur began to receive daily requests to treat other bite-victims. Because he was in Arbois for the summer, however, and was not ready to begin a full-scale rabies service, he had to "abandon them to their fate." After he returned to Paris in September, he decided to treat a second boy whose plight touched him. Jean-Baptiste Jupille, a 15-year-old shepherd from a town near Arbois, had been bitten by a mad dog while protecting several younger boys. At the end of October, a week after treatment had begun on Jupille, Pasteur presented papers to the Academy of Sciences and the Academy of Medicine describing the technique of attenuation using dried rabbit spinal cords and announcing the cures of Meister and Jupille. He ended with a stirring account of Jupille's heroism. He did not, however, divulge how little work he had done on animals before treating the boys. Some physicians questioned his method and his judgment in applying it, but most people cared about only one thing: Pasteur was a savior of innocent children.

Although Pasteur did not perform injections because he was not a medical doctor, popular images often showed him wielding a syringe. Here the saintly bon pasteur (good shepherd) protects children and fur-capped Russians from rabid dogs and wolves.

Temple for a Scientific Saint

After Pasteur announced at the Academy of Sciences that he had successfully treated Joseph Meister for rabies, the president of the Academy declared that Pasteur's achievement "is one of the greatest advances that has ever been accomplished in medicine." Another member of the Academy exclaimed, "rabies, that terrible disease, against which all attempts at therapy up until now have failed, has finally found a cure!" Considering that treatment had only just begun on a second patient, Jupille, and that it was not known whether either boy would have contracted rabies if left untreated, these triumphant statements seem remarkably premature.

Nevertheless, word quickly spread that Pasteur had developed a cure for rabies, and bite victims began to come to Paris from all over France and from abroad. Pasteur's laboratory became an assembly line for inoculation of rabies vaccine. Every morning at 11 o'clock, the patients would line up to receive their injections from Dr. Grancher as

Pasteur looked on (later, three other physicians joined the inoculating team). Nineteen Russians who had been mauled by a wolf brought an exotic flair to the laboratory with their fur hats and thick beards. An Englishman whose hand had been bitten by a black cat spent much of his time in Paris getting drunk; one day he missed an inoculation because he fell into the Seine River. Treatment of the four boys from Newark, New Jersey, sent over to Paris on a ship after being bitten by a mad dog, sparked extensive press coverage and made Pasteur a celebrity in the United States. In the first month following the announcement of the vaccine, 68 people were inoculated; by October 1886, a year later, the numbers had swelled to 2,490, from 18 different countries.

There were a few failures—patients who died. These incidents prompted Pasteur to modify his technique, and they also provided fodder for his critics. The first death was that of Louise Pelletier, a 10-year-old girl who had been very badly bitten on the head over a month before she was brought in for treatment. Three of the wolf-bitten Russians also died, as did the drunk Englishman. Pasteur decided that in serious cases (deep bites to the head or face), the patients would receive intensive treatment. Instead of one daily inoculation of increasingly virulent virus for two weeks, these patients received three or more shots per day for three days. The whole series was then repeated once or twice more with a break of a few days between series. Pasteur chided Roux and Grancher for timidity when they were reluctant to undertake such drastic measures, but after several deaths that critics blamed on this method, he himself recommended a more moderate procedure.

The first months were a period of trial and error for mastering a delicate process. Pasteur visualized the treatment as a race: "Rabies, with its relatively slow incubation period, is like a local train; the vaccine overtakes it like an express train, and, after having overtaken it, keeps it from entering into the body." If the vaccine express were too sluggish, it would not overtake the rabies local. If too forceful, it would hurtle down the tracks, and destroy instead of protect.

Was the rabies vaccine a success? Trying to answer that question led to a great deal of wrangling between Pasteur and his critics. In his report of October 1886, one year after the initial announcement, Pasteur declared that of 1,700 vaccinated people from France and Algeria (occupied by the French since the 1830s), only 10 had died after being treated. This gave a mortality rate of one half of 1 percent. In contrast, if untreated, about one out of six people bitten by a rabid animal would contract the disease and die. Pasteur had saved more than 200 people from a terrible death! Nonsense, replied his critics. No one had ever heard of so many cases of rabies in France before. The annual mortality rate was only 30 to 45. Obviously most of the people Pasteur treated had not been bitten by rabid animals. Pasteur's treatment had made little difference in the total number of people who died of rabies each year, they claimed. Pasteur's side received a boost with the publication of the report of an official committee established in England to assess the rabies vaccination. The report concluded that the treatment was indeed effective; but it also remarked that rabies could be prevented by controlling stray animals rather than vaccinating people after they had been bitten. Although an exact evaluation of Pasteur's rabies treatment can

Pasteur's opponents cast doubts on the safety of the rabies vaccine. The caption of this cartoon reads: "You say, doctor, that your new vaccine against rabies still carries some risk . . . Here's an idea . . . What if you inoculate my mother-in-law! Then we'll have her bitten by a rabid dog."

POUR LA SCIENCE

— Vous dites, Docteur, que votre nouveau vaccin préventif contre la rage offre encore certains aléas. . . . Une idée : . . . . . Si vous inoculiez belle-maman!. . . On la ferait ensuite mordre par un chien enragé.

never be made, most scholars now believe that it did save lives, although not as many as Pasteur and his allies claimed.

A more serious criticism blamed the rabies vaccine for actually causing disease. Some of the people promoting this view were antivivisection and antivaccination activists who distrusted any form of medical intervention. The prominent English antivivisectionist Frances Power Cobb, for instance, in an article entitled "Whither Is Pasteurism to Lead Us?" asked,

> Are we . . . our oxen, our sheep, our pigs, our fowls . . . all to be vaccinated, porcinated, equinated, caninized, felinized, and bovinated, once, twice, 20 times in our lives, or in a year? Are we to be converted into so many living nests for the comfortable incubation of disease germs?

The head of a French antivivisection society, Madame Huot, wrote a letter to Pasteur proposing that she and her son come to his laboratory, allow themselves to be bitten by a rabid dog, and then cure themselves without being vaccinated. Pasteur did not reply.

Pasteur could ignore these activists, but he could not ignore criticism from within the established medical community. The primary spokesman for this group of skeptical physicians was Michel Peter—a distant relative of Marie Pasteur—who launched a sustained attack on Pasteur in the meetings of the Academy of Medicine. Although the conflict became personal, it also reflected a larger-scale clash between traditional medicine, which focused on patients and their symptoms, and the new medicine, which focused on the laboratory. Peter constantly contrasted Pasteur's lack of medical training with his own clinical experience. Pasteur publicly called Peter incompetent because he had never performed a single experiment; privately, he reviled his opponent as loathsome and conceited. Even little Camille, Pasteur's granddaughter, took part in bashing her grandfather's enemies. Pasteur proudly described to his son how one evening at dinner six-year-old Camille had put her fork down, crossed her arms, and announced that if she encountered the people who were opposing Pasteur's treatments, "I know what I would tell them. It would be brief, but would give me lasting pleasure—I would turn my back on them."

Pasteur himself turned his back on Paris for a few months, spending the winter of 1886–87 at a villa in northern Italy with his wife. From there, however, he kept up a constant correspondence with the physicians Grancher and Vulpian, who presented his arguments at the Academy of Medicine. In his biography of his father-in-law, René Vallery-Radot criticized the slanderous people whose harassment kept Pasteur, who was ill and worn out, from enjoying a restful interlude in Italy. But actually Pasteur, as always, thrived on controversy. "The fight is giving me new spirit," he wrote to Grancher's wife. He only wished that Grancher shared his temperament. "May he also find good health in defending truth against envy and pride."

Pasteur prevailed over Peter at the time, but in hindsight, it is possible to see that some of Peter's criticisms were just. He rightly contended that Pasteur had not tested the vaccine adequately on dogs before turning to humans, and that Pasteur had jumped to conclusions too quickly after only two cases, those of Meister and Jupille. He was probably also right when he warned that Pasteur's intensive treatment was dangerous. It was later found that people could develop paralysis after being injected with nerve tissue from animals. A few deaths probably resulted from this side effect. Rabies vaccine is now produced without nerve tissue and uses killed rather than live rabies virus, to guard against the possibility that the vaccine itself might induce rabies. Pasteur, afraid that any bad publicity would hinder people from seeking treatment, would not admit the possibility of complications, and he even helped to hush up one suspicious case by allowing Roux to lie about it. The case concerned the death of a young patient, Édouard-Jules Rouyer, whose father threatened to sue Pasteur when his child died after undergoing treatment. According to Pasteur's nephew Adrien Loir, Roux discovered that the boy had in fact died of rabies but kept these results secret. The cause of the boy's death was officially listed as kidney failure. Dr. Peter was suspicious, but he could never prove that the autopsy report was phony.

In February 1887, Pasteur and his wife returned to Paris from Italy, after having been shaken out of their villa by an earthquake. It had been a scary moment: René and Marie-Louise, with their daughter Camille and their new child Louis, had been visiting. At dawn on Ash Wednesday, the house shook violently. Madame Pasteur, who had risen early to go to church, stood paralyzed as everyone ran into the room and onto Pasteur's bed, where they clutched each other tight and waited for the end. The building stayed intact, but they decided to leave.

Pasteur returned to Paris to discover that he was being turned into a monument, even as he himself began to fade in strength. Plans for the Pasteur Institute, which would become one of the world's leading medical research institutes, were rapidly advancing. "The radiance that his works have shed on our country is incomparable, and now French science is in the first rank," proudly declared his friend Vulpian during a session of the Academy of Medicine. Pasteur's students and colleagues were energetically extending his research program. On the popular level, newspapers and magazines never tired of showering praise on him. He became known in France as *Le bon Pasteur*—the good pastor (minister), or shepherd—a play on words that expressed in condensed form the image of Pasteur as a Christlike savior of children and animals alike.

No opposition, no matter how reasonable, could fight this powerful current. Peter's criticisms were washed away into obscurity, just as Vulpian had predicted during his remarks at the Academy of Medicine meeting: "Our works and names will be lost before long in the rising tide of oblivion; the name and works of M[onsieur] Pasteur will continue to blaze on heights so elevated that they will never be reached by those dreary waves."

No sooner had Pasteur suggested that there was a need for a central facility to take care of the thousands of bite-victims expected to make the pilgrimage to Paris than plans began for construction of the Pasteur Institute. The Institute was set up not as a governmental agency but as a private facility funded by charitable contributions. It was to be a center for rabies treatment, for research on other infectious diseases, and for teaching. Word spread that donations were being accepted, and money quickly flowed in from all over the world, from rich and poor alike, for what newspapers called the "Rabies Palace." Many of the contributions made Pasteur's heart swell—international gifts from the czar of Russia and the emperor of Brazil; and a collection spearheaded by newspapers in Alsace-Lorraine, Joseph Meister's home region, in the name of the first rabies patient. Pasteur's former student Duclaux, who oversaw the construction of the Institute, picked out a large vacant site on the southwest edge of the city. Architects designed an elegant stone building that could have been mistaken for an aristocratic mansion except for the tall chimneys and animal cages.

Although Pasteur took a keen interest in setting up the institute and finding top-notch researchers to head its five divisions, his deteriorating health made him largely a bystander and figurehead. In October 1887, a second stroke paralyzed his tongue. At first mute, he regained his voice, but his speech remained weak and slurred. Although he walked every day with his son-in-law, he needed a lot of rest, and he could not write easily. Still, he undertook one last project: a plan for exterminating rabbits.

Australia and New Zealand had been overrun by the rodents, which had been imported from Europe and were destroying sheep-grazing pastures. Pasteur found out about

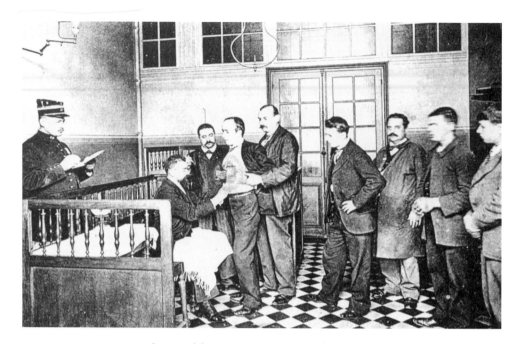

By 1935, more than 51,000 patients had received rabies vaccinations at the Pasteur Institute. The uniformed man keeping records is Jean-Baptiste Jupille, the shepherd who had been one of the first patients to receive Pasteur's vaccine.

the problem one evening when Madame Pasteur was, as usual, reading the newspaper to him. He immediately perked up when he heard that the government of New South Wales was offering an award of 625,000 francs (an enormous sum—about 25 times Pasteur's yearly pension) for anyone who could discover how to exterminate the rabbits. Pasteur mentally added the prize money to the Institute's funds, confident that it would be his. The rabbits would be destroyed through biological warfare. Pasteur proposed spreading food infected with chicken–cholera microbes (fatal for rabbits as well as chickens) where the rabbits would find and eat it, return to their burrows to die, and pass the infection on to their fellow rabbits. Pasteur's nephew Adrien Loir traveled to Australia with two English physicians and a flask full of chicken cholera, but government officials, who were skeptical of the plan, did not allow the release of the germs. The incident was frustrating for Pasteur; communicating over such a long distance was difficult, and his emissaries did not act with the quickness and forcefulness he wished. "Your letters are maddeningly terse," he wrote to the

Australian team. "'The rabbits in Australia are the same as those in France,' what does that mean? Obviously they don't have eyes in the back of their heads. What experiments have been done? On how many rabbits? How long does it take them to die? . . . Certainly you have plenty of time."

The Pasteur Institute was inaugurated in November 1888, in a grand opening ceremony attended by the president of France, Pasteur's fellow Académie Française members, and a host of other politicians and scientists. In his remarks, read by his son, Pasteur regretted having to enter the building as a man "vanquished by time." He urged his collaborators and students to uphold rigorous standards of scientific proof. Their reward would be to attain certainty, "one of the greatest joys that can be felt by the human soul." Pasteur and his wife moved into comfortable apartments in one wing of the new building. A few years later, Joseph Meister and Jean-Baptiste Jupille, the boys whose treatment for rabies had brought Pasteur the worldwide fame that had made the institute possible, came to work as guards there.

As Pasteur aged, he relied more and more on the strong pillars he had erected around himself. On one side, he leaned on devoted disciples, known as the "Pasteurians," who carried on his work and his name. On the other, he relied on the essential support of his family, particularly Madame Pasteur, his "guardian angel," for keeping up his correspondence and caring for him physically and emotionally. He saw Marie-Louise and René every day and doted on his grandchildren, Camille and Louis. Jean-Baptiste and Jeanne, posted in Rome and later Copenhagen, came to Paris as often as they could. Still, Pasteur missed his work: A chemist out of the laboratory, he had written once, is like a soldier without a weapon. The difficulty he had walking, talking, and writing sometimes overwhelmed him with sadness, and he regretted that he had never been able to return to the subject of molecular asymmetry, which had brought

Pasteur at the beach with his grandchildren, Louis and Camille, in 1891. Louis later became a physician and devoted much effort to collecting his grandfather's letters and manuscripts.

Pasteur at the beach with his grandchildren, Louis and Camille, in 1891. Louis later became a physician and devoted much effort to collecting his grandfather's letters and manuscripts.

him so close to solving the ultimate mystery of life. At the end of 1892, he tried a promising new remedy for aging developed by the physiologist Charles Brown-Séquard: injections with extract from the testicles of guinea pigs and dogs. The treatment, which had reportedly rejuvenated other old men, did not seem to have much effect. His lined face, bordered with a thick white beard and topped by a black-rimmed skullcap or bowler, looked tired and melancholy.

An event at the end of 1892 briefly cheered him up: On his 70th birthday, December 27, he was honored with a grand jubilee celebration at the Sorbonne. Scientists and dignitaries from all over France and the world attended, filling the ornate auditorium in their ceremonial robes.

Pasteur shuffled in slowly on the arm of Sadi Carnot, president of France. In his brief remarks, delivered by his son, he pronounced his belief that science and peace would triumph over ignorance and war. To the young in the audience, he urged, "live in the serene peace of laboratories and libraries." Considering the verbal wars he had engaged in, this statement might seem strange. But to Pasteur, the battlefields of science had no relation to those of politics or war. He thought of science as floating in a pure world of truth far above sordid struggles for power, even though his own successes owed much to strategic alliances and militaristic conduct.

Although he could no longer contribute to research himself, and the rabbit project had disappointingly fizzled to nothing, Pasteur was at least able to witness and appreciate an important consequence of the germ theory, the first development that promised to benefit large numbers of people. In 1894, Roux and Alexandre Yersin, working at the Pasteur Institute, developed a treatment for diphtheria,

The president of France escorts Pasteur onto the stage at the Sorbonne at his 70th birthday jubilee. Approaching with open arms is the surgeon Joseph Lister, whose antiseptic techniques had been inspired by Pasteur's work on bacteria.

one of the major killers of young children. Until this time, critics could rightly point out that the germ theory had made little difference for general health and welfare. Mortality after surgery had decreased, but that trend had begun before anyone knew about germs. Rabies, although now preventable, had killed very few people. A possible treatment for tuberculosis had failed to work. In 1892, Robert Koch had announced the discovery of a cure for the disease, an extract from the tuberculosis bacterium called tuberculin. Masses of people had come to Berlin for treatment—only to discover that it was ineffective and could even be harmful. Where were the promised benefits? With the diphtheria treatment, concrete results seemed to be in hand. Pasteur exulted in Roux's success, but because of his lasting grudge against Germany, he refused to come to the ceremony at the Pasteur Institute honoring the German Emil von Behring, whose work had also been vital in developing the technique.

During his last year, Pasteur descended into death by gentle steps, always surrounded by his circle of family and friends. An illness during the winter of 1894–95 kept him in bed for three months. In April he was carried to the institute for a last visit to the laboratory, where he looked through the microscope at the plague bacillus that Alexandre Yersin had isolated in Hong Kong. In June he left the institute to spend the summer at Villeneuve l'Étang, an annex of the Pasteur Institute in a park west of Paris, where the horses used for making diphtheria serum were stabled. He spent most of his days sitting in the garden, where his wife and daughter read him biographies and memoirs of the Napoleonic Wars. He died at the age of 73, on September 28, 1895, from a final stroke.

Pasteur received the funeral of a national hero. His body lay in state at the Pasteur Institute, where people thronged to see it, and crowds lined the streets of Paris for the funeral

text continued on page 115

DIPHTHERIA SEROTHERAPY

Diphtheria used to be one of the most common childhood diseases, and it killed half of those it infected. The sick child's throat became sore and constricted with a "false membrane" that looked like dirty white velvet. Sufferers could hardly swallow or breathe, and doctors often performed tracheotomies (cutting a hole in the throat so that air could enter the windpipe). Death occurred from suffocation or heart failure. Treatments listed in an 1883 American home medical guide included gargling with kerosene, black snakeroot, or lemon juice; drinking dilute sulfuric acid; or applying rubber dissolved in oil to the outside of the throat. The house or apartment was to be filled with the fumes of burning sulfur as a disinfectant.

During the 1880s and 1890s, a number of scientists including Émile Roux and Alexandre Yersin in Paris and Emil von Behring and his Japanese colleague Shibasaburo Kitasato in Berlin, worked out a radically new and more effective treatment, diphtheria serotherapy. Roux and Yersin determined that diphtheria bacteria killed by means of a toxin, a poisonous compound, that they secreted. Behring and Kitasato discovered that bacterial toxins could be combated by means of antitoxins produced in the blood of animals inoculated with the bacteria. Roux and Yersin then applied this method to diphtheria.

The treatment relies on the same principle as that of the rabies vaccine, but with a twist. With the rabies or anthrax vaccines, the injection of a weakened disease agent stimulates the body to become immune (or, as we now understand, to develop antibodies to the disease). In serotherapy, or serum treatment, an animal is vaccinated and made immune to the disease, and its blood serum (the watery part of the blood) is then injected into a person. Instead of developing their own immunity, patients borrow the immunity developed by the animal.

In 1894, after Roux announced the success of the treatment, which he had tested in a Parisian children's hospital, he was bombarded with letters and requests for serum. Diphtheria was such a common disease that the demand was huge, and a French newspaper spearheaded a

DIPHTHERIA SEROTHERAPY

campaign to pay for the horses and serum production. Horses were used as serum factories because large amounts of blood could be taken from them. The institute provided 50,000 doses to doctors within the first three months. Mortality rates from diphtheria fell significantly during the 1890s, for example from 0.61 per thousand in 1894 to 0.34 per thousand in 1900 in London—more than 1,000 fewer deaths. Scholars now believe that the reasons for this drop include other factors in addition to the introduction of serotherapy, such as a change in the diphtheria bacterium to a less virulent form. Still, serotherapy gave doctors a new tool—thanks to the laboratory.

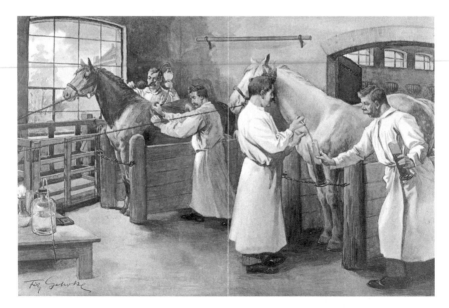

After the announcement of the success of antidiphtheria serotherapy, a national fund-raising campaign was organized. The Pasteur Institute used the money to build stables and purchase about 100 horses, which were immunized and then bled to obtain serum.

text continued from page 112

procession to Notre Dame Cathedral. Newspapers printed sentimental engravings of the great scientist surrounded by garlands of flowers, adoring women, dogs, rabbits, and guinea pigs. One cynical journalist viewed the events with scorn: "The honors rendered to great men . . . are becoming a bit excessive it seems to me; perhaps they are becoming heirs to what used to belong to God." Most everyone else, though, joined in the exaltation. An ornate tomb was built at the Pasteur Institute. Every day, Marie Pasteur walked the short distance from her apartment in the institute down to the crypt. There, under the colorful mosaic scenes from Pasteur's life, with the angels of Faith, Charity, Hope, and Science watching over her, she knelt on the floor next to her husband for a few moments. In the laboratories all around his grave site, his disciples studied microbes. Twenty years before his death, in a passionate plea for the importance of science, Pasteur had written of the laboratory as the temple of the future. Now he lived on in spirit as the saint of the sacred institute he had founded.

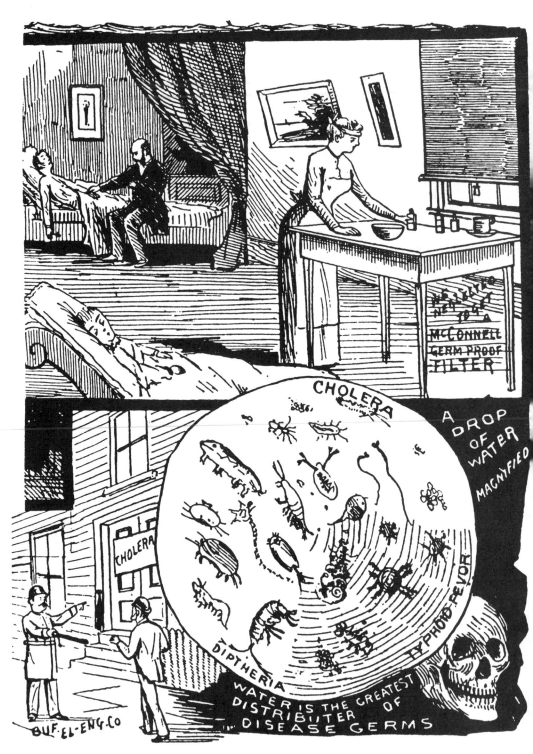

Many manufacturers took advantage of the growing public fear of germs. This 1894 American advertisement suggests that a "germ-proof" water filter would prevent illnesses caused by microscopic creatures (shown in an imaginary enlargement) found in the municipal water supply.

After Pasteur

By the 1890s, the microbes that had been brought onto the stage by Louis Pasteur, Robert Koch, and their colleagues and students had taken on starring roles. Even though most people never actually saw these microscopic organisms, in their mind's eye they could now visualize the tiny creatures' incessant activity, bringing both good and ill to the world. Vintners could imagine yeasts at work in their wine casks, farmers could imagine anthrax bacteria multiplying inside their sheep's distended bellies, surgeons could imagine deadly microbes trying to invade their incisions, and city dwellers could imagine germs jumping out at them from every gob of spit or dirty doorknob.

With this change in conception came new ways of manipulating the natural world. The action of beneficial yeasts and bacteria in producing wine, beer, cheese, soy sauce, and other fermented food products could be better controlled, while unwanted microbes could be destroyed by pasteurization. Today, industrial fermentation is used for purposes ranging from sewage treatment to production of chemicals such as ethanol, glycerol (used in explosives), and lactic acid.

An even greater transformation took place in ways of understanding, preventing, and curing disease. Many diseases came to be seen not as changes within the body produced by a complex interaction between the external and internal environment, but as the result of an invasion by a particular type of microbe. Even physicians at the time were aware that the ground was shifting under them. "[Pasteur] aims at nothing less than to completely overturn our science," charged Jules Guérin, the surgeon who a few months later challenged Pasteur to a duel during one of the heated debates at the Academy of Medicine. So far he had listened to Pasteur's ideas in silence, explained Guérin at a session of the Academy of Medicine in 1880, but now he felt compelled "to defend what I believe to be the fundamentals of medicine against the invasions of the theory of germs." Traditional physicians were no match for Pasteur and his fellow germ-theory combatants. A mere 15 years later, in 1895, another French physician conceded defeat in an editorial published in a medical journal. "Today [Pasteur's] army holds all the keys of the fortress," he wrote. "Diagnosis . . . will soon no longer be able to do without the microscope, bacteriological or chemical analysis, cultures, inoculations, in a word everything that may give our clinical judgments absolutely precise data. . . . We should no longer laugh at bacilli and culture media. . . . We must march with the times. The coming century will see the blossoming of a new medicine: let us devote what is left of this century to studying it." The germ theory had uprooted medicine from its place by the patient's side and planted it in a new location, the laboratory.

Changes in ideas about the causes of disease affected techniques of prevention, although less radically than might be expected. The hygiene movement was already in full swing by the time the germ theory came along: Water was being purified, sewers built, and slaughterhouses cleaned up. With the new theory, though, came a different rationale for cleanliness and a shift in emphasis. Earlier in the 19th century, disease was thought to be conveyed by foul smells. The germ theory held that odors were dangerous only when they betrayed the presence of disease organisms, and that many germs were odorless as well as invisible. Or, as the dean of the Paris Faculty of Medicine, Paul Brouardel, said during the 1880 debate on odors in Paris, "not everything that stinks kills; and not everything that kills stinks." Where once a nose had been enough to detect danger, now a microscope was necessary. One group of people affected by this new view was housewives, who were considered responsible for the health of their families. Doctors and public health officials constantly exhorted them to keep their homes free of dust and dirt and to teach their children rules of hygiene.

Treatment of disease was truly revolutionized by the germ theory. Beginning with Pasteur's rabies vaccine, new discoveries kept making headlines. According to historian Bert Hansen, public attitudes toward medicine changed dramatically during the 1890s. Before that time, the public did not expect doctors to cure many diseases. Suddenly, researchers developed remedies or preventive vaccines for rabies, then diphtheria, whooping cough, typhoid, and a score of other diseases. The successes of modern medicine seemed to be bringing joyful sunshine into the dank, dark realm of death and disease. Identify the germ, create a vaccine, and the scourge is vanquished. After vaccinations became routine in the developed world, parents no longer expected diseases to snatch away their young children. With the introduction in the 1930s and 1940s of sulfa drugs and antibiotics, which inhibited or killed bacteria after they had invaded the body, physicians gained tools to wield against strep throat, pneumonia, and many other possibly fatal infections.

At the same time that Western medicine was conquering germs, Westerners were also conquering distant parts of the world. The two conquests were closely connected. When Europeans traveled abroad, especially to the tropics, they suffered from diseases that were rare or unknown in the Northern Hemisphere, especially malaria, yellow fever, and sleeping sickness. Africa had even earned the nickname "white man's grave." Disease had put a stop to several colonial ventures. One of the most ambitious was a French plan to build a canal between the Caribbean Sea and the Pacific Ocean, through the Isthmus of Panama. The deaths of over 5,000 workers from disease, along with financial difficulties, forced the French to give up the project. It was finally completed by the United States, in 1914, after malaria and yellow fever had been brought under control.

Other French efforts abroad were more successful, aided by the efforts of the growing network of Pasteur Institutes, established to promote medical research in locations scattered around the globe. In the "scramble for Africa" of the 1890s, the French, who had occupied Algeria since the 1830s, expanded their empire to include vast expanses of the western and central parts of the African continent. Indochina (the area that is now Vietnam, Laos, and Cambodia) also came under French control. Along with French political power came French medical expertise. At Pasteur Institutes in the colonies, researchers studied diseases common in the tropics. Charles Nicolle, working in Tunisia, found that

Father Guerlac, a Catholic missionary in Vietnam, accompanied Alexandre Yersin, the founder of the Pasteur Institute at Nha Trang, in his explorations of the region. Missionary work often went hand in hand with colonization.

body lice transmitted typhus, and Alexandre Yersin, based in Nha Trang (Vietnam), discovered the bacterium that causes bubonic plague. As a result, Africa and Southeast Asia became safer for Western colonizers. France was not the only country to link imperialism and medicine. Germany founded the Koch Institute for Infectious Disease, England the Lister Institute, and the United States the Rockefeller Institute, all of which funded studies on tropical diseases.

The triumphal era of the germ theory began to fade in the second half of the 20th century, contributing to a general sense of disillusionment with modern medicine. One reason for this loss of optimism was that germs themselves fought back or resisted control efforts. Strains of bacteria resistant to antibiotics evolved, threatening to disable one of modern medicine's strongest weapons. The 1980s and 1990s saw the reemergence of diseases that had long been kept at bay, such as tuberculosis and hepatitis. Worst of all, the fearsome scourge of AIDS gripped the world and continues to evade the efforts of hundreds of scientists and millions of dollars. By 1995, it was estimated that almost 20 million people worldwide had been infected with HIV, the virus that causes AIDS.

Along with these changes in disease itself came a reassessment of the history of medical progress. Responsibility for improved human health could not be claimed solely by the germ theory, argued many scholars. Figures showed that mortality rates had already started decreasing before the development of vaccinations and antibiotics, probably because of better nutrition and such public health initiatives as clean water and improved sanitation. Health officials realized that in many parts of the world, people were suffering from diseases that could be easily prevented or treated—obstacles to improved health were political and economic, not scientific. Scholars in the developing world questioned the story that Western medicine was a purely beneficial import; they pointed out that many diseases had been brought or spread by Westerners to begin with, that local healing practices had been ignored, and that research on tropical diseases often benefited the colonizers more than it did the native populations.

Like the germ theory, Pasteur's reputation at first shone brilliantly but then began to lose some of its glitter toward the end of the 20th century. For many decades after his death, Pasteur enjoyed the kind of extravagant praise that had previously been reserved for religious saints. During the late 19th and early 20th centuries, science seemed to many people to promise salvation from misery, and scientists such as Pasteur became popular heroes. Like a saint, Pasteur was buried in an ornate tomb and had disciples who pledged to continue his work. His relics (glassware and instruments) were preserved in the same way that pieces of bone or locks of hair from saints once had been. Museums were created at his birthplace in Dole and his home in Arbois, and his room in the institute was preserved as it had been at his death. Almost every town and city in France named a street after him, and a village in Algeria had its name changed to "Pasteur." An unconfirmed story of martyrdom even circulated concerning Joseph Meister, Pasteur's first rabies patient. It was said that during the Second World War, when the German army occupied Paris, Meister, who had become a guard at the Pasteur Institute, intercepted German soldiers at the entrance to Pasteur's tomb, refused them access, and then returned to his room and committed suicide.

The British scientist Stephen Paget asserted in a 1910 article that "[Pasteur] was the most perfect man who has ever entered the Kingdom of Science." Part of the reverence for Pasteur involved listing his admirable characteristics: patriotism, love of family, dedication to science, selflessness, lone genius, and compassion for innocent children and animals. As the wife of a "saint" in the public's perception, Madame Pasteur shared in her husband's glory, being portrayed as the perfect companion.

The Pasteur "cult" lived on for a long time and continues to some extent today. In the late 20th century, though, Pasteur's reputation had begun to be reassessed. This has to do partly with the recognition of the limitations of the germ theory, and also for other reasons. For one thing, scholars are less interested now in adulating famous people—even scientists—as perfect heroes or heroines, and more willing to see their human failings. Certain traits ascribed to Pasteur are now recognized as either false or exaggerated. Selfless? No. Pasteur enjoyed doing research, had a huge ego, and loved recognition. Compassionate? Yes, but his wish to benefit humanity was always mixed with desire for personal glory. Love of family? As long as they agreed to play second fiddle to his work. Sole genius? Not quite. His contributions came more through persistence than flashes of insight, and he relied heavily on collaborators and family members for material and intellectual support. Other traits that were denied or excused by his family and colleagues—arrogance, combativeness, opportunism, and secretiveness—have been acknowledged by his recent biographers.

Changing values have also affected assessments of Pasteur's character. Some attributes that used to be considered positive do not seem so admirable anymore. Pasteur's ultra-patriotism now looks petty and narrow rather than noble. His dominance within his family is also no longer very appealing. Few people now would praise Madame Pasteur's self-effacement in the way that her son-in-law did in a lecture in 1913: "Never thinking of herself, she did not want anyone to pay attention to her. The word 'I' . . . was so foreign to her vocabulary that, during the thirty years during which I had the pleasure of living near her, of loving and venerating her, I do not remember ever hearing her utter a sentence that began with that word."

Pasteur's reputation has also suffered from the release of his laboratory notebooks, which were not available for scholars to study until the 1970s. (He had requested that they be destroyed, but they were preserved by his grandson and donated to the Bibliothèque Nationale de France [French National Library]). In 1995, Gerald Geison, a professor at Princeton University, published a book titled *The Private Science of Louis Pasteur.* Based on close analysis of Pasteur's notebooks, Geison concluded that Pasteur had been dishonest in his public pronouncements about some of his most well-known experiments and concluded that "we need no longer perpetuate Pasteur's image of himself."

Although the book received generally positive reviews, it sparked a blistering attack from Max Perutz, a distinguished biochemist, in the *New York Review of Books.* Pasteur, Perutz wrote, was "a good and just man who cannot defend himself because he is dead." He acknowledged some of Pasteur's minor flaws, but accused Geison of trying to topple a truly great man from his pedestal. "Pasteur may have been domineering, intolerant, pugnacious, and, in his later years, a hypochondriac who searched every slice of bread for bacteria before eating it; but he was courageous, compassionate, and honest, and his scientific achievements, which have much reduced human suffering, make him one of the greatest benefactors of mankind."

Despite such defenders, Pasteur's days as a saintly hero are probably over, and rightly so. But it is nonetheless remarkable that he achieved fame both for himself and the world of "infinitesimally small beings" by following a path he laid out, when he was only 17, in a letter to his sister: "Action and work always follow will, and work is almost always accompanied by success. These three things—will, work, and success—make up all of human existence: will opens the door to a brilliant and happy career, work allows one to walk through this door, and after one has arrived at the end of the journey, success comes to crown one's achievement."

CHRONOLOGY

1822
Born to Jean-Joseph Pasteur and Jeanne-Étiennette Roqui in Dole, December 27

1827
Family moves to Arbois

1838
Returns to Arbois after one month in Paris preparatory school; draws pastels

1839–42
Studies at Collège Royal de Franche-Comté, Besançon, receives bachelor of science degree August 13, 1842

1842–43
Resides in Paris at Barbet Institution; takes classes at Collège Saint Louis

1843–47
Studies at École Normale Supérieure, Paris; receives doctorate August 28, 1847

1847–57
Studies crystallography; discovers structure of racemic acid

1849
Begins work as professor of chemistry at Faculty of Sciences, Strasbourg, in January; marries Marie Laurent May 29

1854
Begins work as professor of chemistry and dean of Faculty of Sciences, Lille, in December

1857
Appointed Administrator and Director of Scientific Studies at École Normale Supérieure, Paris, in October

1859

Daughter Jeanne dies, September 10

1857–65

Investigates role of microorganisms in fermentation; does experiments to disprove doctrine of spontaneous generation

1862

Elected to Academy of Sciences, December 8

1865–66

Deaths of father (June 15, 1865) and two daughters (Camille, September 11, 1865; Cécile, May 23, 1866)

1866

Publication of *Studies on Wine*

1867

Loses job at École Normale Supérieure after student walk-out; appointed professor of chemistry at the Sorbonne

1865–70

Studies silkworm diseases

1868

Stroke on October 19 leaves Pasteur's left side partially paralyzed

1870

Publication of *Studies on Silkworm Diseases*

1870–71

Franco-Prussian War; Pasteur family flees occupied Paris

1871–77

Further studies on fermentation and spontaneous generation

1874

Awarded a National Reward (lifetime salary) by National Assembly, July 12

1876
Publication of *Studies on Beer*

1877–95
Studies infectious diseases in animals and humans

1881
Trial of anthrax vaccine at Pouilly-le-Fort, June 2; election to Académie Française, December

1885
Treatment of Joseph Meister with rabies vaccine begins July 6

1888
Founding of Pasteur Institute on November 14

1895
Dies at Villeneuve-l'Étang on September 28

acid
Chemical substance that contains a hydrogen atom, reacts with bases to form salts, and usually tastes sour.

antisepsis
Preventing infection by killing or inhibiting the growth of microorganisms.

asepsis
Preventing infection by keeping out microorganisms (for example from an operating room).

atom
The smallest unit of an element, consisting of a nucleus surrounded by electrons.

attenuation
Reducing the virulence (strength) of a microorganism.

bacteriology
The study of bacteria.

bacterium (plural **bacteria**)
A group of one-celled organisms that have no distinct boundary separating the nucleus from the cytoplasm and multiply by splitting in two.

cell
The fundamental microscopic unit of all living things, consisting of a nucleus and cytoplasm surrounded by an enclosing membrane.

contagious disease
A disease that is transmitted by direct or close contact.

crystal
A solid that has a regularly repeating arrangement of atoms.

crystallography
The science of crystals.

enzyme
A type of molecule naturally occurring in plants and animals that speeds up chemical reactions without itself being altered or destroyed.

fermentation
An energy-yielding chemical reaction in which organic compounds are broken down incompletely, that is, not all the way to carbon dioxide and water. Different types of fermentation are named for the compounds that result from them, for example alcohol, lactic acid, butyric acid, acetic acid, and citric acid fermentations.

fungus (plural **fungi**)
A group of nongreen plants, including molds, mushrooms, and yeasts.

germ
Microorganism; or, small bit of living matter that can develop into an organism.

germ theory of disease
The theory that some diseases (especially contagious diseases) are caused by microorganisms.

germ theory of fermentation
The theory that life processes carried on by microorganisms cause fermentation in nature.

immunity
The condition of being able to resist a disease, usually because of having been exposed to the disease before or because of having been vaccinated against it.

infectious disease
A disease transmitted by microorganisms.

microbe
Microorganism.

microbiology
The study of microbes.

microorganism
A living being so small that it can be observed only through a microscope; includes viruses, bacteria, and microscopic fungi or parasitic organisms.

molecule
A chemical unit made up of one or more atoms.

parasite
An organism that lives on or in another organism from which it draws its nourishment.

polarized light
Light whose waves vibrate only in one plane, instead of in all directions.

salt
A compound that results when the hydrogen atom from an acid is replaced with a metal or a positively charged group of atoms.

serotherapy
Treatment of an infectious disease by injection of serum (the watery portion of blood, excluding red blood cells and other solids) containing compounds that neutralize the disease agents.

stereochemistry
The study of the spatial arrangement of atoms in the structure of a molecule.

trephination
Removal of a small piece of the skull.

vaccine
A preparation, usually a killed or attenuated microbe, that confers immunity against a disease. Originally referred to vaccination of cowpox to protect against smallpox.

virus
An infective agent consisting of genetic material surrounded by a protein coat, which cannot grow independently of living cells. Until the late 19th century, used for any invisible "poison" thought to cause disease.

vivisection
Scientific experimentation on living animals, usually involving a cutting operation.

yeast
Microscopic one-celled fungi, many of which carry out fermentation.

MUSEUMS
AND HISTORIC
PLACES

Pasteur Museum at Institut Pasteur

25, rue du Docteur Roux, 75015 Paris
Phone: 33.(0)1.45.68.82.83
Closed in August
www.pasteur.fr

Pasteur's living quarters have been preserved as they were when he and Madame Pasteur lived at the institute. A scientific gallery has Pasteur's laboratory instruments on display. Visitors can also see the crypt containing the tombs of Louis and Marie Pasteur.

Pasteur Museum of Research Applications in Marnes

3, avenue Pasteur, 92430 Marnes La Coquette
Phone: 33.(0)1.47.01.15.97
Closed in August

Pasteur and his colleagues carried out research on rabies at this site (Villeneuve l'Etang), just west of Paris. The museum contains exhibits about the work of Pasteur, Roux, and their successors, and the room where Pasteur died has been preserved.

Société des amis de la maison natale de Pasteur

43, rue Louis Pasteur
F-39000 Dole, Franche-Comté
Phone: 33.(0)3.84.72.20.61
Closed on Tuesdays.

This house, Pasteur's birthplace, contains exhibits of Pasteur memorabilia, including some of the pastel drawings he did when young and some scientific instruments.

Maison de Louis Pasteur

83, rue de Courcelles
39600 Arbois, Franche-Comté
Phone: 33.(0)3.84.66.11.72
Open April 1 to October 15; closed on Tuesdays.
www.acad-sciences.fr/fondations/pasteur.html (Web page in French)

This museum is in the house where Pasteur grew up and later spent vacations and did research on wine. Contains the original furniture and laboratory.

Musée Yersin Institut Pasteur de Nha Trang

8, Tran Phu
Nha Trang, Vietnam
Phone: 84.5.882.9540
www.pasteur.fr

This museum honors the work of Alexandre Yersin, who founded the Pasteur Institute in Vietnam and was one of the discoverers of the bubonic plague bacillus. It contains exhibits and Yersin's room, with the original furnishings.

Jenner Museum

High Street
Berkeley, Gloucestershire, GL13 9BH
England
Phone: 44.(0)1.453.810631
Open April to September and Sundays in October
www.fivevalleys.demon.co.uk/jenner.htm

This museum, in Edward Jenner's home, contains exhibits on the development of the smallpox vaccine.

FURTHER READING

Works by Pasteur Available in English

Pasteur, Louis, and Joseph Lister. *Germ Theory and Its Applications to Medicine and On the Antiseptic Principle of the Practice of Surgery.* Amherst, N.Y.: Prometheus, 1996.

Pasteur, Louis. *Studies on Fermentation: The Diseases of Beer, Their Causes, and the Means of Preventing Them.* Trans. Frank Faulkner and D. Constable Robb. 1879. Reprint, New York: Kraus, 1969.

Conant, James Bryant. *Pasteur's Study of Fermentation.* Cambridge: Harvard University Press, 1952. [Includes translation of Pasteur's 1857 article on lactic fermentation.]

Pasteur's Life and Work

Debré, Patrice. *Louis Pasteur.* Trans. Elborg Forster. Baltimore, Md.: Johns Hopkins University Press, 1998.

Dubos, René J. *Louis Pasteur: Free Lance of Science.* 1950. Reprint, New York: Scribners, 1976.

Duclaux, Émile. *Pasteur: The History of a Mind.* Trans. Erwin F. Smith and Florence Hedges. 1920. Reprint, Metuchen, N.J.: Scarecrow, 1973.

Geison, Gerald L. "Louis Pasteur." In *The Dictionary of Scientific Biography,* ed. Charles C. Gillispie, vol. 10: 350–416. New York: Scribners, 1974.

Geison, Gerald L. *The Private Science of Louis Pasteur.* Princeton, N.J.: Princeton University Press, 1995.

Latour, Bruno. *The Pasteurization of France.* Trans. Alan Sheridan and John Law. Cambridge: Harvard University Press, 1988.

Perutz, M. F. "The Pioneer Defended." Review of Gerald L. Geison, *The Private Science of Louis Pasteur. New York Review of Books,* Dec. 21, 1995. Response by Geison and reply to response by Perutz in *New York Review of Books,* April 4, 1996.

Vallery-Radot, René. *The Life of Pasteur.* Trans. Mrs. R. L. Devonshire. Garden City, N.Y.: Garden City Publishing, 1926.

Chemistry, Microbiology, and Medicine

Arnold, David. "Medicine and Colonialism." In *Companion Encyclopedia of the History of Medicine,* ed. W. F. Bynum and Roy Porter, pp. 1393–1416. London: Routledge, 1993.

Baker, Robert. "The History of Medical Ethics." In *Companion Encyclopedia of the History of Medicine,* ed. W. F. Bynum and Roy Porter, pp. 852–87. London: Routledge, 1993.

Baxby, Derrick. *Jenner's Smallpox Vaccine: The Riddle of Vaccinia Virus and Its Origin.* London: Heinemann Educational Books, 1981.

Brock, Thomas D. *Robert Koch: A Life in Medicine and Bacteriology.* Madison, Wisc.: Science Tech Publishers, 1988.

Bulloch, William. *The History of Bacteriology.* 1938. Reprint, New York: Dover, 1979.

Bynum, W. F. *Science and the Practice of Medicine in the Nineteenth Century.* Cambridge: Cambridge University Press, 1994.

Coleman, William. *Biology in the Nineteenth Century: Problems of Form, Function, and Transformation.* New York: Wiley, 1971.

Curtin, Philip D. *Death by Migration: Europe's Encounter with the Tropical World in the Nineteenth Century.* New York: Cambridge University Press, 1989.

De Kruif, Paul. *Microbe Hunters.* New York: Harcourt, Brace, 1926.

French, Richard D. *Antivivisection and Medical Science in Victorian Society.* Princeton, N.J.: Princeton University Press, 1975.

Fruton, Joseph S. *Molecules and Life: Historical Essays on the Interplay of Chemistry and Biology.* New York: John Wiley, 1972.

Hansen, Bert. "America's First Medical Breakthrough: How Popular Excitement about a French Rabies Cure in 1885 Raised New Expectations for Medical Progress." *American Historical Review* 103 (April 1998): 373–418.

Hughes, Sally Smith. *The Virus: A History of the Concept.* New York: Science History Publications, 1977.

La Berge, Ann F. *Mission and Method: The Early Nineteenth-Century French Public Health Movement.* New York: Cambridge University Press, 1992.

Lechevalier, Hubert A., and Morris Solotorovsky. *Three Centuries of Microbiology*. 1965. Reprint, New York: Dover, 1974.

Parish, H. J. *Victory with Vaccines: The Story of Immunization*. Edinburgh/London: E. & S. Livingstone, 1968.

Ramsay, O. Bertrand. *Stereochemistry*. London: Heyden, 1981.

Reid, Robert. *Microbes and Men*. New York: Saturday Review Press, 1975.

Spink, Wesley W. *Infectious Diseases: Prevention and Treatment in the Nineteenth and Twentieth Centuries*. Minneapolis: University of Minnesota Press, 1978.

Tomes, Nancy. *The Gospel of Germs: Men, Women, and the Microbe in American Life*. Cambridge: Harvard University Press, 1998.

19th-Century France

Crosland, Maurice. *Science under Control: The French Academy of Sciences, 1795–1914*. New York: Cambridge University Press, 1992.

Paul, Harry W. *From Knowledge to Power: The Rise of the Science Empire in France, 1860–1939*. New York: Cambridge University Press, 1985.

Popkin, Jeremy D. *A History of Modern France*. Englewood Cliffs, N.J.: Prentice Hall, 1994.

Weisz, George. *The Medical Mandarins: The French Academy of Medicine in the Nineteenth and Early Twentieth Centuries*. New York: Oxford University Press, 1995.

ACKNOWLEDGMENTS

I thank Michael Shank for connecting me with Oxford. Kristin Bray, Libbie Freed, Frederick C. Robbins, Alice N. Robbins, Alison Sandman, Juliet Skuldt and members of her writing class, Mary Tebo, and Nancy Toff provided helpful comments.

**PICTURE
CREDITS**

AKG, London: 114; Bibliothèque Nationale de France: 63, 82; Bouvet Collection: 103; Historical Collections of the College of Physicians Phildelphia: 116; Insitut Pasteur: frontispiece, 8, 13, 14, 16, 20, 22, 25, 29, 31, 40, 43, 45, 48, 50, 52, 56, 58, 64, 68-69, 72, 74, 77, 80, 86, 93, 95, 98, 100, 108, 110, 111, 115, 120, 123; Library of Congress: 36-37; Wellcome Library, London: 89

Louise Robbins is a writer and editor. Her forthcoming book is entitled *Elephant Slaves and Pampered Parrots: Exotic Animals in Eighteenth Century Paris.* She received her doctorate in the history of science from the University of Wisconsin—Madison.

Middle School of Plainville LIC
Plainville, CT